Chemical Kinetics

© Inner London Education Authority 1984

First published 1984
by John Murray (Publishers) Ltd
50 Albemarle Street
London W1X 4BD

Reprinted 1985, 1988, 1990

Printed and bound in Great Britain by
St Edmundsbury Press Ltd, Bury St Edmunds, Suffolk

British Library Cataloguing in Publication Data

Independent Learning Project for Advanced
    Chemistry
    Chemical Kinetics. – (ILPAC; Unit P5)
    1. Science
    I. Title   II. Series
    500   Q161.2

    ISBN 0-7195-4043-7

27/05/92

CONTENTS

PREFACE   v
Acknowledgements   vi
Key to activity symbols and hazard symbols   vii

INTRODUCTION   1

Pre-knowledge   2
PRE-TEST   3

LEVEL ONE   5

THE RATE OF A REACTION   5
The decarboxylation of 2,4,6-trinitrobenzoic acid   5
Evaluating reaction rate   7
RATE EQUATIONS, RATE CONSTANTS AND ORDERS OF REACTION   9
Summary   11
Using rate equations   12
Experimental methods   13
Experiment 1 - investigating the hydrolysis of benzenediazonium chloride 15
Half-life of first order reactions   19
The order of reaction with respect to individual reactants   21
Experiment 2 - the kinetics of the reaction between iodine and
               propanone in aqueous solution   24
COMPUTER-AIDED REVISION   29
LEVEL ONE CHECKLIST   30
LEVEL ONE TEST   31

LEVEL TWO   37

REACTION MECHANISMS   37
Molecularity   37
The rate-determining step   38
Proposing a reaction mechanism   39
The hydrolysis of halogenoalkanes   42
ACTIVATION ENERGY AND THE EFFECT OF TEMPERATURE ON REACTION RATE   44
The fraction of particles with energy greater than E_a 46
The Arrhenius equation   48
Using the Arrhenius equation   48
Experiment 3 - determining the activation energy of a reaction   50
CATALYSIS   52
Catalysts and activation energy   53
Autocatalysis   55
Experiment 4 - determining the activation energy of a catalysed reaction 56
THE COLLISION THEORY   57
THE TRANSITION STATE THEORY   60
Energy profiles and the transition state theory   60
LEVEL TWO CHECKLIST   61

END-OF-UNIT TEST   63

APPENDIX ONE   67

NOTES ON TANGENTS AND THEIR SLOPES   67
Drawing tangents   67
Negative and positive slopes   68
A note on 'differential notation'   69
INTEGRATED RATE EQUATIONS   70
First order reactions   71
Second order reactions   72

APPENDIX TWO   73

'CLOCK' REACTIONS   73
Experiment 5 - a bromine 'clock' reaction   74

ANSWERS TO EXERCISES   78

PREFACE

This volume is one of twenty Units produced by ILPAC, the Independent Learning Project for Advanced Chemistry, written for students preparing for the Advanced Level examinations of the G.C.E. The Project has been sponsored by the Inner London Education Authority and the materials have been extensively tested in London schools and colleges. In its present revised form, however, it is intended for a wider audience; the syllabuses of all the major Examination Boards have been taken into account and questions set by these boards have been included.

Although ILPAC was initially conceived as a way of overcoming some of the difficulties presented by uneconomically small sixth forms, it has frequently been adopted because its approach to learning has certain advantages over more traditional teaching methods. Students assume a greater responsibility for their own learning and can work, to some extent, at their own pace, while teachers can devote more time to guiding individual students and to managing resources.

By providing personal guidance, and detailed solutions to the many exercises, supported by the optional use of video-cassettes, the Project allows students to study A-level chemistry with less teacher-contact time than a conventional course demands. The extent to which this is possible must be determined locally; potentially hazardous practical work must, of course, be supervised. Nevertheless, flexibility in time-tabling makes ILPAC an attractive proposition in situations where classes are small or suitably-qualified teachers are scarce.

In addition, ILPAC can provide at least a partial solution to other problems. Students with only limited access to laboratories, for example, those studying at evening classes, can concentrate upon ILPAC practical work in the laboratory, in the confidence that related theory can be systematically studied elsewhere. Teachers of A-level chemistry who are inexperienced, or whose main discipline is another science, will find ILPAC very supportive. The materials can be used effectively where upper and lower sixth form classes are timetabled together. ILPAC can provide 'remedial' material for students in higher education. Schools operating sixth form consortia can benefit from the cohesion that ILPAC can provide in a fragmented situation. The project can be adapted for use in parts of the world where there is a severe shortage of qualified chemistry teachers. And so on.

A more detailed introduction to ILPAC, with specific advice both to students and to teachers, is included in the first volume only. Details of the Project Team and Trial Schools appear inside the back cover.

LONDON 1983

ACKNOWLEDGEMENTS

Thanks are due to the following examination boards for permission to reproduce questions from past A-level papers:

Oxford Delegacy of Local Examinations;

    Exercise 17(1977)
    Level One Test 8(1980)

Southern Universities Joint Board;

    Exercise 45(1978)

The Associated Examining Board;

    End-of-Unit Test 2(1981)

University of Cambridge Local Examinations Syndicate;

    Exercise 20(1983)

University of London Entrance and School Examinations Council;

    Exercises 15(1983), 16(1979), 18(1972), 19(1975), 25(1979),
          26(1972), 27(1975), 30(N1975), 35(N1982), 36(N1977)
    Level One Test 1(N1974), 2(1977), 3(N1977), 4(N1975), 5(N1977),
            6(N1978), 7(1979), 9(N1981), 10(1974), 11(1976),
            12(N1976)
    End-of-Unit Test 1(1976), 5(N1980)
    Teacher-marked Exercise p61(1973)

Welsh Joint Education Committee;

    End-of-Unit Test 3(1977), 4(1975)

Questions from papers of other examining boards appear in other Units.

Where answers to these questions are included, they are provided by ILPAC and not by the examination boards.

Exercise 9 is reproduced, by permission, from Nuffield Advanced Science: Chemistry; Students' Book II (1st edition), edited by B.J. Stokes and published by Longman Group Limited for the Nuffield Foundation.

Experiment 5 is based, with the permission of Longman Group Ltd., on an experiment which appeared in 'An Experimental Introduction to Reaction Kinetics' by M.A. Atherton and J.K. Lawrence (0582 32145 X).

Photographs are included by permission as follows:

Fig. 16 (page 48): Svante Arrhenius - Geoff Cox, by courtesy of the Royal
                                Society of Chemistry.

Photographs of students and Fig. 17 (page 51) - Tony Langham.

SYMBOLS USED IN ILPAC UNITS

 Reading

 Exercise

 Test

 'A' Level question

 'A' Level part question

 'A' Level question
Special paper

 Worked example

 Teacher-marked exercise

 Revealing exercise

 Discussion

 Computer programme

 Experiment

 Video programme

 Film loop

 Model-making

INTERNATIONAL HAZARD SYMBOLS

 Harmful

 Flammable

 Corrosive

 Toxic

 Explosive

 Oxidising

 Radioactive

INTRODUCTION

If you have studied Unit 03 (More Functional Groups) you will have come across the oxidation of ethanal by acidified dichromate(VI) ions:

$$3CH_3CHO(aq) + Cr_2O_7^{2-}(aq) + 8H^+(aq) \rightarrow 3CH_3CO_2H(aq) + 2Cr^{3+}(aq) + 4H_2O(l)$$

How does this reaction take place? Does it seem likely, for example, that three ethanal molecules, one dichromate(VI) ion and eight hydrogen ions would all collide at the right moment and burst apart again, to give three ethanoic acid molecules, two chromium(III) ions and four water molecules?

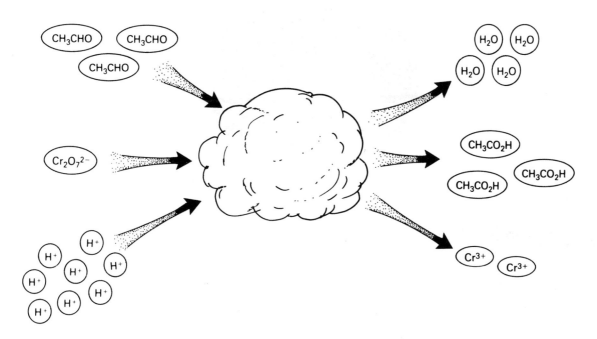

Fig.1.

No - it's extremely unlikely that twelve particles would collide like this - even though the equation for the reaction might seem to suggest that they do. The stoichiometric equation for a reaction is the sum of all the processes that take place. It doesn't show how they take place (the mechanism), how many separate reaction steps there may be in the reaction, or how many molecules are involved at each stage.

In this Unit, we aim to show how experimental studies of rates of reaction under different conditions can be used to work out possible mechanisms for reactions. By mechanism, sometimes called reaction pathway, we mean the series of separate steps that go to make up a reaction.

In Level One we look at the experimental side. We show you how to analyse data to get a rate equation and scan the different methods available for measuring reaction rates.

In Level Two we show how you can work out a mechanism from a rate equation, look at the effect of temperature on chemical reactions and finally examine briefly two theories of reaction rates - the collision theory and the transition state theory.

In Appendix One, we show you various ways of constructing a tangent to a curve, and we also consider some of the mathematics which you may encounter in text-books concerned with reaction rates.

There are five experiments in this Unit: two in Level One, two in Level Two and one in Appendix Two.

There is an ILPAC video-programme designed to accompany this Unit; it is divided into two sections. It is not essential, but you should try to see it at the appropriate times if it is available.

Reaction kinetics

PRE-KNOWLEDGE

Before you start work on this Unit, you should be able to:

(1)   state that a rate is a change in some quantity with time;

(2)   list the variety of ways in which the rate of a chemical reaction can be measured, e.g., by reference to changes in mass, volume or concentration of reactant or product;

(3)   find the rate of a reaction, given the slope of a graph of the measured variable (as in (2)) against time;

(4)   state the effect of the following on the rate of a chemical reaction -

   (a)   change in concentration of reactants

   (b)   change in surface area of reactants

   (c)   change in temperature

   (d)   the presence of a catalyst.

PRE-TEST

To find out whether you are ready to start Level One, try the following test which is based on the pre-knowledge items. You should not spend more than thirty minutes on this test. Hand your answers to your teacher for marking.

1. Some high speed trains are supposed to cruise at a speed of 125 miles per hour (miles hr^{-1}). Which of the following units could also be used to express the speed of a train?

    A m^{-2} B $km\ hr^{-1}$ C $miles\ min^{-1}$ D $ft\ s^{-1}$ E $m\ min^{-2}$ (1)

2. Which of the following units could be used to express the rate of the reaction between magnesium and hydrochloric acid?

    $$Mg(s) + 2HCl(aq) \rightarrow H_2(g) + MgCl_2(aq)$$

    A $cm^{-3}\ s$ C $mol^2\ dm^{-6}\ hr^{-1}$ E $mol\ dm^{-3}\ min^{-1}$

    B $cm^3\ min^{-1}$ D $cm^3\ s^{-1}$ (1)

3. The following information concerns an experiment to investigate the rate of reaction between calcite (a form of calcium carbonate) and excess hydrochloric acid. 1.05 g of calcite reacted with 10 cm^3 of 2 M hydrochloric acid in a small flask. The flask was weighed at two minute intervals to determine the loss in mass due to the evolution of carbon dioxide. The results were recorded in the form of the graph below. In this graph the loss in mass is plotted against the time from the moment when the two substances were mixed. Use this graph to assist you in answering the following questions.

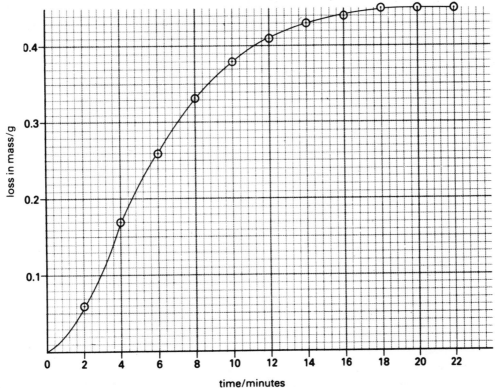

Fig.2.

(a) What mass of carbon dioxide has been formed nine minutes from
     the start of the reaction?   (1)

(b) During which one of the following two minute intervals was the
     reaction quickest?

        (i)   0 to 2 minutes

       (ii)   8 to 10 minutes

      (iii)   2 to 4 minutes

       (iv)   16 to 18 minutes   (1)

(c) After how many minutes had just half of the calcite reacted? (1)

(d) What was the maximum mass of carbon dioxide formed?   (1)

(e) What fraction of a mole of carbon dioxide is this?   (1)

(f) What fraction of a mole is 1.05 g of calcium carbonate?   (1)

(g) Write the equation for the reaction between calcium carbonate
     and hydrochloric acid. (C = 12.0, O = 16.0, Ca = 40.0)   (2)

4 5 g of granulated zinc is put in a conical flask and covered with
   100 cm³ (an excess) of 2 M hydrochloric acid at 20 °C. A fairly
   slow reaction takes place.

   For each of the following changes state whether you would expect the
   rate to be increased, decreased or unchanged and give a reason for
   your answer.

   (a) 5 g of powdered zinc is used instead of granulated zinc.

   (b) 3 g of granulated zinc is used instead of 5 g.

   (c) 100 cm³ of 2 M ethanoic (acetic) acid is used instead of hydro-
        chloric acid.

   (d) The temperature is raised to 40 °C.

   (e) A few drops of aqueous copper(II) sulphate is added.   (10)

                                              (Total 20 marks)

4

LEVEL ONE

The study of chemical kinetics (reaction rates) is of importance to industrial chemists because they are concerned with making particular products as economically as possible. Therefore, following the rates of reaction, interpreting them and altering them have important industrial applications as well as improving our understanding of chemistry. These are some of the factors which you consider in Level One.

THE RATE OF A REACTION

Objectives. When you have finished this section, you should be able to:

(1) calculate values for the rate of reaction at various times, from a graph of concentration of reactant against time;

(2) write an equation to show the relationship between rate of reaction and concentration of reactant.

The study of reaction kinetics relies on experimental work. We begin by presenting you with a set of experimental results.

We have chosen a reaction where a single substance (the reactant) breaks down. We will take you through a series of exercises on the data, to show you how to find the rate equation for the reaction. Our purpose is to illustrate the key ideas of reaction rate, order of reaction and rate constant.

The decarboxylation of 2,4,6-trinitrobenzoic acid

2,4,6-Trinitrobenzoic acid in solution loses carbon dioxide when heated, as shown by the following equation:

Since one of the products is gaseous the rate of reaction could be studied by measuring the volume of carbon dioxide produced. Alternatively, you could follow the decrease in the amount of 2,4,6-trinitrobenzoic acid itself.

The scientists who did the experiment in 1931 (E.A. Moelwyn-Hughes and O.N. Hinshelwood) chose the second method. They set up several mixtures at 90 °C. After various reaction times they withdrew a sample and added a large volume of iced water to quench (i.e. stop) the reaction. They then titrated each mixture with 5.0×10^{-3} M barium hydroxide solution using bromothymol blue as indicator.

We have taken the following figures from their results:

Table 1

Time/min	Concentration of 2,4,6-trinitrobenzoic acid/mol dm^{-3}
0	2.77×10^{-4}
18	2.32×10^{-4}
31	2.05×10^{-4}
55	1.59×10^{-4}
79	1.26×10^{-4}
157	0.58×10^{-4}
Infinity	0.00

The first step in analysing this sort of data is to plot a graph of concentration of reactant against time. You do this in the first exercise. Square brackets will be used to denote concentration throughout this Unit, i.e. $[X(aq)]$ = concentration of X in mol dm^{-3} of aqueous solution.

Exercise 1   Plot a graph of concentration of 2,4,6-trinitrobenzoic acid (vertical axis) against time (horizontal axis). Use a large piece of graph paper, as you will have to draw tangents to the curve later and you will need plenty of working space for this.

(Answer on page 78)

You now have a graph showing how concentration of reactant changes with time. The rate of change per unit time (per minute in this case) is given by the slope of the graph. This is the <u>rate of reaction</u>.

In the next exercise you look at your graph to see how much you can learn about the rate of reaction by inspection.

Exercise 2   Place your ruler under the curve at time 0, with the long edge of the ruler hugging the curve. Notice the slope of the ruler. Move the ruler slowly along the curve, checking how its slope changes as you go. Then answer the following questions.

(a) When is the rate of reaction greatest and when is it least?

(b) Suggest one reason why the rate of reaction is changing.

(Answers on page 78)

We now show you how to get a value for the rate of reaction at an instant (instantaneous reaction rate) from a concentration/time curve.

Evaluating reaction rate

In Exercise 2, while moving your ruler along the graph, you were, in fact, comparing the slopes of tangents to the curve at various points.

To get a value for the slope of a graph at a particular point, draw a tangent to the curve at that point and measure the slope of the tangent. In Appendix One (page 67) we suggest several methods which can be used to construct tangents accurately.

A measured slope has a number, a sign and a unit. The number tells how fast the concentration (or some other quantity such as volume of gas) is changing with time. The sign indicates whether the quantity (Y), such as concentration, is increasing or decreasing, as in Fig. 3 below. The unit combines the units of the change being measured (such as concentration) and time.

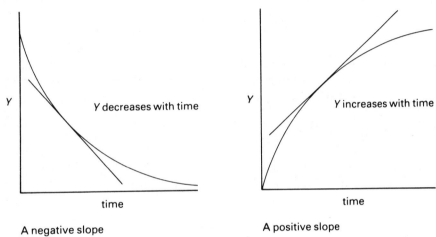

Fig.3.   A negative slope   A positive slope

Rate of reaction is usually defined as the rate of change of magnitude of the concentration of a reactant or a product with time and can be obtained from the slope of the concentration/time graph. In most of the exercises rate will have units of:

$$(\text{concentration}) \times (\text{time}^{-1}) \quad \text{e.g.} \quad \text{mol dm}^{-3} \text{ s}^{-1}$$

However, if a reaction is being followed by a physical method, involving the measurement of, say, mass or volume, the rate can be expressed in corresponding units, such as those of mass time^{-1} (e.g. g s^{-1}) or volume time^{-1} (e.g. cm^3 min^{-1}).

In fact, rate can be expressed in a variety of units, as long as the quantity measured is proportional to the concentration or amount of either a reactant or a product. If rate does have units other than those of concentration time^{-1} it should always be clear from the context.

In the next exercise you calculate the slope and thus the rate of reaction at specified times.

Exercise 3 Take the graph you drew in Exercise 1 and construct
tangents to the curve at 10, 50, 100 and 150 minutes
(using one of the methods given in the Appendix).
Calculate their slopes and complete a copy of Table 2.
Bear in mind that where the slope is negative, the value of the
slope, but not the sign, gives the rate.

Table 2

Time /min	Concentration /mol dm^{-3}	Slope /mol dm^{-3} min^{-1}	Rate /mol dm^{-3} min^{-1}
10			
50			
100			
150			

(Answers on page 78)

You now have a set of figures to show that the rate of reaction for the
decarboxylation of 2,4,6-trinitrobenzoic acid is decreasing with time. The
concentration of reactant is also decreasing with time. What we now want to
know about this reaction is, in what way does the rate of reaction depend on
the concentration of reactant?

A standard way of finding out whether two quantities, say x and y, are
directly related is to plot a graph of y against x . If the graph is a
straight line going through zero, then y is directly proportional to x:

$$y \propto x \qquad \text{or} \quad \frac{y_1}{x_1} = \frac{y_2}{x_2} = \frac{y_3}{x_3} = m$$
$$\text{or} \quad y = mx$$

where m is a constant, equal to the slope of the line. If y is proportional
not to x but to (x + a constant) the equation is:

$$y = mx + c$$

where c is the intercept on the y axis or the value of y when x = 0 (see
Fig. 4).

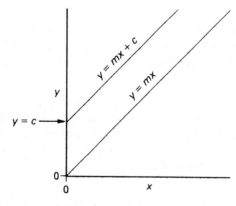

Fig.4.

Now go on to the next Exercise, where you find the relationship between the
rate of the decarboxylation of 2,4,6-trinitrobenzoic acid and its
concentration.

Exercise 4 Plot a graph of rate of reaction (vertical axis) against concentration of 2,4,6-trinitrobenzoic acid (horizontal axis) using your values in Table 2 (Exercise 3). Now answer the following questions:

    (a) Does your graph go through the origin? Explain why it should.

    (b) Use your graph to state the relationship between rate of reaction and concentration of reactant:

        (i) in words

        (ii) mathematically.

  (Answers on page 78)

The expression you have just worked out in Exercise 4 is called the rate equation for the reaction. We consider rate equations in more detail in the next section.

RATE EQUATIONS, RATE CONSTANTS AND ORDERS OF REACTION

A rate equation relates the rate of a reaction to the concentrations of the reacting species by means of constants called (a) the rate constant and (b) the order(s) of reaction.

Objectives. When you have finished this section, you should be able to:

(3) identify the order of reaction with respect to a named reagent;

(4) determine the overall order of reaction;

(5) work out a value for the rate constant of a first order reaction, including its unit;

(6) recognise a first order reaction from a graph of rate against concent-ration of reactant.

Read about rate equations (rate expressions) and rate constants (velocity constants) in your text-book(s). Distinguish carefully between the order of reaction with respect to one reactant and the overall order. Some books use the 'differential notation' for the rate of reaction, e.g.

$$\text{rate of reaction} = -\frac{d[\text{reactant}]}{dt}$$

You will find this easy if you study mathematics but we suggest you need not use it in this context since it is rarely required for A-level chemistry. However, if you want some further explanation, look in Appendix One.

We will spend more time on orders of reaction and their uses later in the Unit; at the moment you should be able to apply what you have just learned to the rate equation for the decarboxylation of 2,4,6-trinitrobenzoic acid. You do this in the next Exercise.

Exercise 5   Use the rate equation which you worked out in Exercise 4
              to state:

(a)   the order of reaction with respect to 2,4,6-trinitro-
      benzoic acid;

(b)   the overall order of reaction.

(Answers on page 78)

You should be able to work out a value for the rate constant for a first
order reaction like this one, both graphically and by substituting into the
rate equation. To make sure you can use both methods, try the next two
exercises.

Exercise 6   Using both your graph and rate equation from Exercise 4,
              work out a value for the rate constant (k) of the
              decarboxylation of 2,4,6-trinitrobenzoic acid at 90 °C.

What is the unit of the rate constant for this reaction?

(Answer on page 78)

Another method to calculate the rate constant is to substitute values of rate
and concentration (from your graph) into the rate equation, rearranged to
give:

        k = rate/concentration

and average the results. Try this in the next exercise.

Exercise 7   (a)   Use your graph from Exercise 1 to calculate a value
                    for the rate of reaction at zero time (the initial
                    rate).

(b)   Calculate the rate constant (k) for each of the
      times (10, 50, 100 and 150 minutes) listed in Table 2 and
      for zero time.

(c)   Average your results.

(Answers on page 79)

In the next exercise, you compare the values of k which you calculated in
Exercises 6 and 7.

Exercise 8   Which of the two values of k that you have just
              calculated is likely to be more accurate? Explain your
              choice.

(Answer on page 79)

All the exercises so far in this Unit have been based on data from the
decarboxylation of 2,4,6-trinitrobenzoic acid. The following summary will
help you to identify the main points in these exercises.

Summary

So far in this Unit, we have shown you how to:

(a) plot a concentration/time curve from experimental data;

(b) draw tangents to this curve and hence calculate values of reaction rate;

(c) use rate/concentration data obtained from this curve to identify a first order reaction by plotting rate versus concentration;

(d) express the relationship between rate and concentration of a reactant mathematically (a rate equation or rate expression);

(e) calculate a value for the rate constant in two ways.

Now try the next exercise, where you are given rate/concentration data for a different reaction and asked to deduce the rate expression, the order of reaction and the rate constant.

Exercise 9   Table 3 contains some data for the decomposition of dinitrogen pentoxide in tetrachloromethane (tcm) solution:

$$2N_2O_5(tcm) \rightarrow 4NO_2(tcm) + O_2(g)$$

Table 3

Concentration of N_2O_5/mol dm^{-3}	Rate of reaction as decrease in concentration of N_2O_5 per second /10^{-5} mol dm^{-3} s^{-1}
2.21	2.26
2.00	2.10
1.79	1.93
1.51	1.57
1.23	1.20
0.92	0.95

Plot a graph of the rate of the reaction against the concentration of N_2O_5, and try to answer these questions:

(a) What is the rate expression for the reaction?

(b) What order is this reaction with respect to N_2O_5?

(c) What is the value of the constant in the rate expression? Include the correct unit.

(Answers on page 79)

In the next section we aim to extend your knowledge of rate equations and orders of reaction to more complicated reactions.

Using rate equations

So far you have studied reactions in which one compound decomposes. We now take a brief look at reactions involving more than one reactant.

Objectives. When you have finished this section, you should be able to:

(7) use a given rate equation to identify the order of reaction with respect to an individual reactant;

(8) use a given rate equation to identify the overall order of reaction;

(9) define order of reaction with respect to an individual reactant and overall order of reaction.

To see that you have understood the difference between overall order and order of reaction with respect to a single reactant, try the following three short exercises.

Exercise 10   The reaction between mercury(II) chloride and ethanedioate ions takes place according to the equation:

$$2HgCl_2(aq) + C_2O_4{}^{2-}(aq) \rightarrow 2Cl^-(aq) + 2CO_2(g) + Hg_2Cl_2(s)$$

The rate equation for the reaction is

$$\text{rate} = k\,[HgCl_2(aq)][C_2O_4{}^{2-}(aq)]^2$$

(a) What is the order of reaction with respect to each reactant?

(b) What is the overall order of reaction?

(Answers on page **79**)

In the next exercise you may be surprised to find a fractional order in the rate equation. You will not come across fractional orders very often at A-level, but you should be aware that they exist and are a sign of a more complex reaction mechanism than the ones you will be investigating in Level Two.

Exercise 11   For the following reaction:

$$C_2H_4(g) + I_2(g) \rightarrow C_2H_4I_2(g)$$

the rate equation is:

$$\text{rate} = k\,[C_2H_4(g)][I_2(g)]^{3/2}$$

(a) What is the order of reaction with respect to each reactant?

(b) What is the overall order of reaction?

(Answers on page **79**)

The next exercise deals with the overall order of a hypothetical reaction.

Exercise 12   Substances P and Q react together to form products and
the overall order of reaction is three. Which of the
following rate equations could not be correct?

A   rate = k [P]^2[Q]

B   rate = k [P]^0[Q]^3

C   rate = k [P][Q]^2

D   rate = k [P][Q]^3

E   rate = k [P][Q]^2[H$^+$]^0

(Answer on page 79)

Now do the next exercise, to check that you can work out units for the rate
constant, k, for a reaction which is not first order.

Exercise 13   The equation for the reaction between peroxodisulphate
ions and iodide ions is:

$$S_2O_8{}^{2-}(aq) + 2I^-(aq) \rightarrow 2SO_4{}^{2-}(aq) + I_2(aq)$$

The rate equation is:

$$rate = k\ [S_2O_8{}^{2-}(aq)][I^-(aq)]$$

If concentrations are measured in mol dm^{-3} and rate in
mol dm^{-3} s^{-1}, determine the unit of k. Show your working
clearly.

(Answer on page 79)

We now go on to consider the various ways in which reactions can be followed
to collect information for kinetic studies.

Experimental methods

In the decarboxylation of 2,4,6-trinitrobenzoic acid, the reaction was
followed by a titration method. This is a straightforward technique, but
has the disadvantage that the reaction mixture is destroyed in the process.

Many other methods are available for measuring the rate of reaction. We
take a look at the more important of these physical methods which all share
the advantage that they do not interfere with the reaction mixture in any
way.

Objectives. When you have finished this section you should be able to:

(10) choose suitable methods for measuring the rates of different types of
reaction;

(11) describe in outline each of the main methods for measuring reaction
rate.

Read about the different methods that are commonly used to measure reaction rates. We suggest that you make brief notes on the following methods: sampling and titration; measuring gas volume; polarimetry; colorimetry; conductivity; dilatometry (measuring change in volume of liquids). The video-programme mentioned below would also be useful.

For each method you should consider the type of reaction that could be followed by it, and an outline of how it works.

At this point you should watch part 1 of the ILPAC video-programme 'Chemical Kinetics' if it is available. This part of the tape gives details of all the methods of measuring reaction rates listed above.

Now attempt the next exercise.

Exercise 14   For each of the following reactions, decide which method or methods (there may be more than one) you could use to monitor its progress.

(a) $CaCO_3(s) + 2HCl(aq) \rightarrow 2CaCl_2(aq) + CO_2(g) + H_2O(l)$

(b) $2MnO_4^-(aq) + 5C_2O_4^{2-}(aq) + 16H^+(aq) \rightarrow 2Mn^{2+}(aq) + 8H_2O(l) + 10CO_2(g)$

(c) $(CH_3)_3CBr(l) + H_2O(l) \rightarrow (CH_3)_3COH(aq) + H^+(aq) + Br^-(aq)$

(d) $CH_3CH(OC_2H_5)_2(aq) + H_2O(l) \rightarrow CH_3CHO(aq) + 2C_2H_5OH(aq)$

(e) $H_2O_2(aq) + 2I^-(aq) + 2H^+(aq) \rightarrow 2H_2O(l) + I_2(aq)$

(f) $C_{12}H_{22}O_{11}(aq) + H_2O(l) \rightarrow C_6H_{12}O_6(aq) + C_6H_{12}O_6(aq)$
        sucrose   glucose   fructose

(Answers on page 79)

Now attempt the following Teacher-marked Exercise. You may want to look over your notes before starting. When you have finished, hand it to your teacher for marking.

Teacher-marked   Review the methods that are available for measuring
Exercise   the rates of chemical reactions. For each method
you should mention: (a) what is being measured,
(b) for what type of reaction it is suitable, and
(c) brief details of apparatus (no diagrams needed).

Now that you have looked at the various different methods of measuring reaction rates, do Experiment 1, where you follow the rate of hydrolysis of benzenediazonium chloride using a physical method - measuring the volume of nitrogen produced.

EXPERIMENT 1

An investigation of the hydrolysis of benzenediazonium chloride

Aim

The purpose of this experiment is to determine the rate equation for the reaction in which benzenediazonium chloride is hydrolysed and hence find the order of reaction with respect to benzenediazonium chloride.

Introduction

Benzenediazonium chloride is an unstable substance, which decomposes when heated above 5 °C to give phenol, nitrogen and hydrochloric acid:

$$C_6H_5N_2{}^+Cl^-(aq) + H_2O(l) \rightarrow C_6H_5OH(aq) + N_2(g) + HCl(aq)$$

There are several stages in the preparation of the reaction mixture, so you do this at a temperature low enough for the rate of reaction to be negligible. When you are ready, you warm the mixture quickly to a fixed temperature and measure the volume (V_t) of gas produced at one minute intervals for about 25 minutes. You then leave the mixture until no further reaction appears to be occurring, and measure the total volume (V_∞) of gas produced since the clock was started.

Because the volume of gas produced in time t is proportional to the amount of benzenediazonium chloride used up, it follows that:

$$V_\infty \propto [C_6H_5N_2{}^+Cl^-(aq)] \text{ at the start}$$

$$V_\infty - V_t \propto [C_6H_5N_2{}^+Cl^-(aq)] \text{ at time } t$$

A plot of ($V_\infty - V_t$) against time will therefore have the same form as the concentration/time graph and can be used to obtain information about the rate of reaction.

Note that, in this experiment, you need not attempt to judge the time when the reaction begins. The clock can be started at any time after the mixture has reached a steady temperature. Even if some benzenediazonium chloride has reacted by then, the amount remaining can be taken as giving the 'initial' concentration, and this can be calculated, if necessary, from V_∞.

$$2MnO_4^{2-} + 5C_2O_4^{2-} + 16H^+ \rightarrow 2Mn^{2+} + 8H_2O + CO_2$$

Requirements

safety spectacles and protective gloves
water bath, thermostatically controlled, set between 40 and 50 °C
thermometer, 0-100 °C
side-arm test-tube with bung
3-way tap
glass syringe, 100 cm³
rubber tubing (2 short lengths)
2 retort stands, bosses and clamps
wash-bottle of distilled water
measuring cylinder, 10 cm³
test-tube
sodium nitrite, $NaNO_2$ — — — — — — — — — — — — — — — — — — —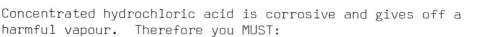
spatula
beaker 250 cm³
crushed ice
hydrochloric acid, concentrated, HCl — — — — — — — — — — — — —
pumice or anti-bumping granules
graduated pipette, 5 cm³ or 10 cm³
pipette filler
phenylamine, $C_6H_5NH_2$ — — — — — — — — — — — — — — — — — —
teat-pipette
stopclock or stopwatch

Hazard warning

Phenylamine is toxic, by ingestion and by skin absorption.
It is also flammable and gives off a harmful vapour.

Concentrated hydrochloric acid is corrosive and gives off a
harmful vapour. Therefore you MUST:

WEAR SAFETY SPECTACLES AND GLOVES
WORK IN A FUME CUPBOARD WHERE POSSIBLE
KEEP BOTTLES AWAY FROM FLAMES
KEEP STOPPERS ON BOTTLES AS MUCH AS POSSIBLE

Procedure

1. Set the control on the water bath to a temperature between 40 and 50 °C
   and hang a thermometer in it. If possible this should be done before the
   lesson so that it has time to reach a steady temperature.

2. Set up the apparatus, without the chemicals, as shown in Fig. 5.

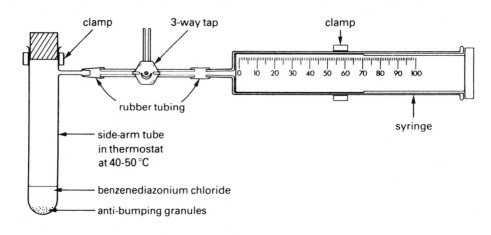

Fig.5.

3. When you have connected the three-way tap between the side-arm tube and the syringe, turn the tap so that it connects the syringe with the open air as in Fig. 6, A. Press the plunger in, so that the syringe is empty, and then turn the tap so that it connects the side-arm tube with the air as in Fig. 6, B.

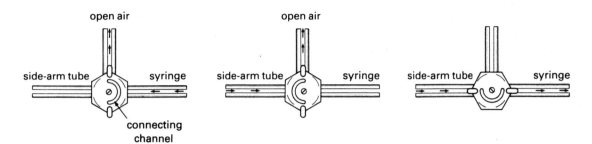

A. Emptying syringe   B. Allowing gas to escape   C. Collecting gas

Fig.6.

4. Using a 10 cm³ measuring cylinder, add 2.0 cm³ of distilled water into a test-tube. Weigh 0.80 g of sodium nitrite and dissolve it in the water. Cool this solution in a beaker of crushed ice and keep it handy.

5. Remove the side-arm tube and, using a measuring cylinder, measure into it 5.0 cm³ of distilled water and 2.5 cm³ of concentrated hydrochloric acid.

6. Add a few anti-bumping or pumice granules to the side-arm tube and seal its mouth with a rubber bung.

7. Place the side-arm tube in a beaker of crushed ice and, using a pipette and filler, add 1.0 cm³ of phenylamine. Mix the contents of the tube thoroughly and allow them to cool.

8. Using a teat-pipette, add the sodium nitrite solution a few drops at a time to the phenylamine solution in the side-arm tube. Shake the tube gently to swirl its contents as you do so.

9. Check that the thermostat temperature has become constant (at about 45 °C), then clamp the side-arm tube in position in the thermostat (see Fig. 5) so that the solution is completely immersed in water.

10. Wait four minutes with the tap open to the air, so that the solution warms to the temperature of the water-bath. Record the temperature.

11. After four minutes, turn the tap so that it connects the side-arm tube with the syringe (Fig. 6, C), reset the clock and take a reading. Regard this as time zero. Don't shake the tube now or hereafter.

12. Continue taking readings each minute for about 25 minutes. Enter your results in a larger copy of Results Table 1. The total volume of gas produced is over 100 cm³, so as you see the volume approaching the 100 cm³ mark, get ready to turn the tap to the position shown in Fig. 6, A (emptying the syringe into the air). Just as it reaches 100 cm³, turn the tap, expel the collected nitrogen, then turn the tap back to the position shown in Fig. 6, C (connecting the side-arm tube with the syringe). Depending on how you make up your mixture, you may have to do this twice during the experiment.

13. After 25 minutes, leave the apparatus for at least another half hour for the reaction to finish completely. This gives you the total volume of nitrogen produced in the reaction, V_{∞} (i.e., the volume produced at infinite time). If you want to speed things up, immerse the side-arm tube into a beaker of hot water at about 60 °C. If the syringe is nearly full, empty it first, noting the volume of nitrogen expelled. The volume of nitrogen should reach its maximum in a few minutes. Remember to allow the syringe to cool back down to the temperature of the waterbath before taking your final reading (V_{∞}).

Results Table 1

Time, t/min								
Volume of N_2, V_t/cm^3								
$(V_{\infty}-V_t)$/cm^3								

(Specimen results on page 80)

Calculations

1. Work out the values of $(V_{\infty}-V_t)$ and enter them into your copy of Results Table 1.

2. Plot $(V_{\infty}-V_t)$ (vertical axis) against time (horizontal axis). Draw a smooth curve through the points.

3. Construct tangents to your curve and measure the slope at each point. Draw one at time 0 and at least four others evenly spaced.

4. Use your graph to complete a larger copy of Results Table 2.

Results Table 2

Time /min	Slope /cm^3 min^{-1}	Rate /cm^3 min^{-1}	$(V_{\infty}-V_t)$/cm^3

(Specimen results on page 80)

5. Plot another graph of rate of reaction against $(V_{\infty} - V_t)$, which is proportional to the concentration of benzenediazonium chloride.

Questions

1. Use the information from your second graph to write a rate equation for the reaction.

2. Use your second graph to work out a value for the rate constant, k, for the reaction, including its units.

3. Explain why the escape of gas during the first four minutes, before recording the first volume reading, can be neglected.

(Answers on page 80)

In the next section we take a look at another aspect of first order reactions.

Half-life of first order reactions

If you are asked to show that a reaction is of the first order you can often do this by calculating its half-life. As you will see, there is only one graph to plot!

You have already come across the idea of half-life of a reaction in Unit S2 (Atomic Structure), in connection with the decay of radioactive isotopes. All radioactive isotopes decay by first order kinetics. The rate equation is -

        rate = k [reactant]

Each radioactive isotope has its own half-life. Since the intensity of the radioactivity of a sample is proportional to the amount of the isotope it contains, the half-life is the time taken for the radioactivity to fall to half its original value.

If you are not sure of the definition of half-life, look it up. Also read about the half-life of first order reactions.

Objectives. When you have finished this section, you should be able to:

(12) define the term half-life;

(13) determine the half-life of a first order reaction from graphical data of concentration versus time;

(14) identify a reaction with a constant half-life as being first order.

To revise the idea of radioactive decay and half-life, try the next exercise.

Exercise 15 (a) State what is meant by the term 'half-life'.

(b) The following is a decay curve for a radioactive element X.

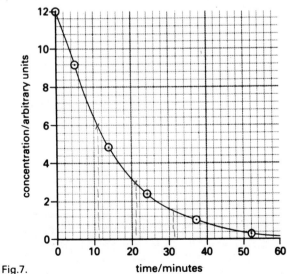

Fig.7.   time/minutes

(i) Determine the half-life of X.

(ii) What is the order of the decay reaction?

(Continued on page 20.)

(c)   On a copy of the axes below, sketch the approximate
        relationship between rate of decay and concent-
        ration of X.

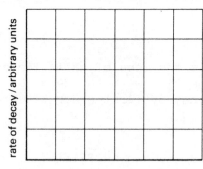

Fig.8.   concentration of X/arbitrary units

(Answers on page **81**)

Other first order reactions, besides radioactive decay processes, have
constant half-lives. You use this fact in the next exercise.

Exercise 16   The following chemical reaction, under certain conditions,
                proceeds with the order shown.

$$2N_2O_5 \rightarrow 4NO_2 + O_2$$ First order

(a)   In one experiment on the reaction, the initial concent-
        ration of N_2O_5 was 32 units and the half-life was 5
        minutes. On a copy of the graph below, plot the relation
        between the concentration of N_2O_5 and time for this
        experiment.

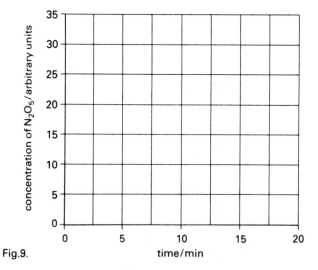

Fig.9.   time/min

(b)   When the reaction was carried out in tetrachloromethane,
        it was found that an initial concentration of N_2O_5 of
        2.00 mol dm^{-3} gave an initial rate of reaction of
        2.10 x 10^{-5} mol dm^{-3} s^{-1}. Calculate the rate constant for
        the reaction and state the units.

(Answers on page **81**)

In the next exercise you apply the half-life concept to the reaction you
considered in Experiment 1.

Exercise 17   The decomposition of benzenediazonium chloride in aqueous
               solution is a reaction of the first order which proceeds
               according to the equation:

$$C_6H_5N_2Cl(aq) \rightarrow C_6H_5Cl(l) + N_2(g)$$

A certain solution of benzenediazonium chloride contains
initially an amount of this compound which gives 80 cm^3 of
nitrogen on complete decomposition. It is found that, at 30 °C,
40 cm^3 of nitrogen are evolved in 40 minutes. How long after
the start of the decomposition will 70 cm^3 of nitrogen have
been evolved? (All volumes of nitrogen refer to the same
temperature and pressure.)

(Answers on page 81)

In the next section we show you how to determine the order of reaction with
respect to one reactant at a time, from experimental data, in a reaction
which involves two or more reactants.

The order of reaction with respect to individual reactants

Objectives.   When you have finished this section, you should be able to:

(15)   determine the order of reaction with respect to individual reactants
       from initial rate data;

(16)   determine the rate equation for the iodination of propanone by
       following the reaction colorimetrically.

We show you how to determine the order of reaction with respect to individual
reactants in the following Worked Example.

Worked Example   The data in Table 4 were obtained for the reaction
                 between nitrogen monoxide and hydrogen at 700 °C.
                 The stoichiometric equation for the reaction is:

$$2H_2(g) + 2NO(g) \rightarrow 2H_2O(g) + N_2(g)$$

Table 4

Experiment number	Initial concentration /mol dm^{-3}		Initial rate /mol dm^{-3} s^{-1}
	H$_2$	NO	
1	0.01	0.025	2.4 x 10^{-6}
2	0.005	0.025	1.2 x 10^{-6}
3	0.01	0.0125	0.6 x 10^{-6}

Determine the order of reaction with respect to NO and to
H$_2$. Write the rate equation for the reaction.

<u>Solution</u>

1. Consider Experiments 1 and 2 in Table 4.

    Initial [NO(g)] is constant. Therefore, any variation in initial rate is due to the variation in initial [H$_2$(g)].

2. Deduce the order of reaction with respect to hydrogen.

    Halving initial [H$_2$(g)] halves the rate of reaction.

    ∴ rate ∝ [H$_2$]^1 i.e. the order with respect to H$_2$ = 1

3. Consider Experiments 1 and 3 in Table 4.

    Initial [H$_2$(g)] is constant. Therefore, any variation in initial rate is due to the variation in initial [NO(g)].

4. Deduce the order of reaction with respect to nitrogen monoxide.

    Halving initial [NO(g)] gives one quarter the rate, i.e. ($\frac{1}{2}$)^2.

    ∴ rate ∝ [NO(g)]^2 i.e. the order with respect to NO = 2

5. Write the rate equation.

    $$\text{rate} = k[\text{H}_2(\text{g})][\text{NO}(\text{g})]^2$$

Use the same method for the following exercises.

<u>Exercise 18</u> Two gases, A and B, react according to the stoichiometric equation:

$$A(g) + 3B(g) \rightarrow AB_3(g)$$

A series of experiments carried out at 298 K in order to determine the order of this reaction gave the following results.

Table 5

Expt.	Initial concentration of A c/mol dm^{-3}	Initial concentration of B c/mol dm^{-3}	Initial rate of formation of AB$_3$ /mol dm^{-3} min^{-1}
1	0.100	0.100	0.00200
2	0.100	0.200	0.00798
3	0.100	0.300	0.01805
4	0.200	0.100	0.00399
5	0.300	0.100	0.00601

(a) What is the order of the reaction between A and B with respect to

     (i) substance A   (ii) substance B?

(b) Write down a <u>rate equation</u> for the reaction between A and B.

(c) Using the experimental data given for Experiment 1, Table 5, calculate the <u>rate constant</u>, k, for the reaction. Give the appropriate units of k.

(Answers on page 81)

Exercise 19   A series of experiments was carried out on the reaction:

$$2H_2(g) + 2NO(g) \rightarrow 2H_2O(g) + N_2(g)$$

The initial rate of reaction at 750 °C was determined by noting the rate of formation of nitrogen, and the following data recorded:

Table 6

Expt.	Initial concentration of nitrogen monoxide/mol dm^{-3}	Initial concentration of hydrogen /mol dm^{-3} s^{-1}	Rate of formation of nitrogen /mol dm^{-3} s^{-1}
1	6.0×10^{-3}	1.0×10^{-3}	2.88×10^{-3}
2	6.0×10^{-3}	2.0×10^{-3}	5.77×10^{-3}
3	6.0×10^{-3}	3.0×10^{-3}	8.62×10^{-3}
4	1.0×10^{-3}	6.0×10^{-3}	0.48×10^{-3}
5	2.0×10^{-3}	6.0×10^{-3}	1.92×10^{-3}
6	3.0×10^{-3}	6.0×10^{-3}	4.30×10^{-3}

The rate equation for the reaction is:

$$\text{rate} = k[H_2]^m[NO]^n$$

Deduce the order of the reaction with respect to

(a)   hydrogen

(b)   nitrogen monoxide.

(Answers on page 81)

In the next experiment you determine a rate equation for the reaction between iodine and propanone in aqueous solution. Since one of the reactants is coloured, you will follow the reaction colorimetrically.

If you do not have access to a reliable colorimeter, your teacher may recommend that you do an alternative experiment, which you will find in Appendix Two.

EXPERIMENT 2

The kinetics of the reaction between iodine and propanone in aqueous solution.

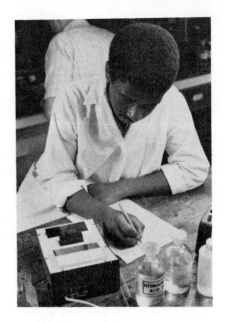

Aim

The purpose of this experiment is to obtain the rate equation for the reaction between iodine and propanone by determining the order of reaction with respect to each reactant and to the catalyst (hydrogen ions). The equation is:

$$I_2(aq) + CH_3COCH_3(aq) \rightarrow$$
$$CH_3COCH_2I(aq) + H^+(aq) + I^-(aq)$$

Introduction

A catalyst does not necessarily appear in the stoichiometric equation (here it appears as a product) but it can appear in the rate equation. The other species which are likely to appear are the reactants and so you may assume that the rate equation is:

$$\text{rate} = k[CH_3COCH_3]^p[I_2]^q[H^+]^r$$

You will be determining the order of reaction with respect to each reactant by varying the concentration of each species in turn, keeping the others constant and following the reaction colorimetrically. As the intensity of the iodine colour decreases more light is transmitted through the solution (i.e. the absorbance decreases).

There are three parts to the experiment:

1. Choosing the right filter for the colorimeter.

2. Calibrating the colorimeter so that meter readings can be converted to concentrations of iodine.

3. Obtaining values for the concentration of iodine at intervals of time for a series of experiments with the following sets of conditions:

    (a) Initial $[CH_3COCH_3]$ varying; $[I_2]$, $[H^+]$ constant

    (b) Initial $[I_2]$ varying; $[CH_3COCH_3]$, $[H^+]$ constant

    (c) Initial $[H^+]$ varying; $[CH_3COCH_3]$, $[I_2]$ constant

    Each set of experiments gives you the order of reaction with respect to one component. If there are three groups of students in your class working on this experiment, then we suggest that each group assumes responsibility for one set of conditions. Sharing your results will speed up matters considerably.

Requirements

safety spectacles
colorimeter with a set of filters
set of optically matched test-tubes to fit colorimeter (with stoppers)
wash-bottle of distilled water
4 burettes with stands, filling funnels and beakers
iodine solution, 0.020 M I_2 (in KI(aq))
propanone solution, 2.0 M CH_3COCH_3
hydrochloric acid, 2.0 M HCl
stopclock or watch
thermometer, 0 to 100 °C

Procedure

1. <u>Choose a filter</u>. First, switch on the colorimeter to allow it to warm up. (Leave it switched on until you have finished, unless your teacher advises otherwise.) Ideally, the filter should let through <u>only</u> light of the particular wavelength absorbed by the coloured solution. So, for a red solution which absorbs cyan light, you would use a cyan filter - cyan is the complementary colour to red (see Fig. 10). Since iodine solution is reddish, use a filter in the blue-green range. To select the best, proceed as follows.

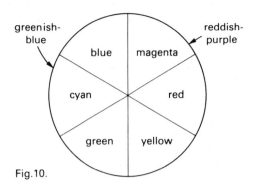

Fig.10.

   (a) Put any one of the suitable filters into the slot in the colorimeter and insert a tube of distilled water, covering it to exclude stray light. Turn the adjusting knob so that the meter shows zero absorbance (or, on some colorimeters, 100% transmission). Mark the rim of the tube so that you can replace it without rotation.

   (b) Replace the tube with a tube containing the most concentrated iodine solution you will use (see Results Table 3) and take a reading of absorbance (or % transmission). Mark this tube too so that you can replace it in the same position (i.e. without rotation).

   (c) Repeat steps (a) and (b) above for other suitable filters in turn.

   (d) Choose the filter which gives the greatest absorbance (or least transmission).

2. Prepare a calibration curve, so that you can convert your meter readings taken during the experiment to concentration of iodine.

   (a) To do this, prepare a series of iodine solutions as suggested in Results Table 3. Measure and record the absorbance of each one. Most colorimeters are liable to 'drift', so you should zero the machine before each reading, by inserting the distilled water 'blank' and re-setting the needle to 100% transmission.

   Results Table 3

Volume of 0.020 M I_2 solution/cm³	Volume of distilled water/cm³	$[I_2(aq)]$ /mol dm⁻³	Meter reading (% absorbance or transmission)
0.0	10.0	0	
1.0	9.0	0.0020	
2.0	8.0	0.0040	
3.0	7.0	0.0060	
4.0	6.0	0.0080	
5.0	5.0	0.010	

   (b) Plot a graph of meter reading against concentration of iodine and keep this to use in analysing your results.

(Specimen results on page 81)

25

3. Decide which series of experiments you will do from Table 7 below and note their letters. The figures in heavy type will help you choose. If no other students are working on this investigation then you will need to do all the experiments.

Table 7

	Experiment						
	a	b	c	d	e	f	g
Volume of 2 M propanone/cm³	2	4	6	2	2	2	2
Volume of 0.02 M iodine/cm³	2	2	2	4	1	2	2
Volume of 2 M HCl /cm³	2	2	2	2	2	4	6
Volume of water /cm³	4	2	0	2	5	2	0
[Propanone] /mol dm⁻³	**0.4**	**0.8**	**1.2**	0.4	0.4	0.4	0.4
[I₂]/mol dm⁻³	**0.004**	0.004	0.004	**0.008**	**0.002**	0.004	0.004
[H⁺]/mol dm⁻³	**0.4**	0.4	0.4	0.4	0.4	**0.8**	**1.2**

4. For your first mixture, measure out iodine solution, acid and water from burettes into a test-tube. Wipe the tube clean and handle only at the top.

5. Measure the propanone solution into another test-tube, again using a burette. Keep the outside of all tubes clean and dry.

6. Adjust the colorimeter to zero against the tube of distilled water.

7. Add the propanone solution to the first mixture and start the clock. Quickly stopper the test-tube and invert it six or seven times to mix the contents thoroughly.

8. Put the tube in the colorimeter in time to take a reading at 30 seconds after the clock was started.

9. Take further readings at 30 second intervals for 6 minutes, or until the colour disappears, if this occurs sooner. Record your results in a copy of Results Table 4.

10. Record the temperature of the room and the temperature of the mixture after the final reading. If they differ by more than 2 or 3 °C you may be advised to repeat the experiment, modifying the procedure as in step 12.

11. Repeat steps 4 to 10 for the other two mixtures in your set of experiments.

12. If time permits, repeat your measurements. Some colorimeters may give better results if you remove the tube after each reading, and reset the meter to zero just before re-inserting the reaction tube in time for the next reading.

Results Table 4

Time/min	0	$\frac{1}{2}$	1	$1\frac{1}{2}$	2	$2\frac{1}{2}$	3	$3\frac{1}{2}$	4	$4\frac{1}{2}$	5	$5\frac{1}{2}$	6
Meter reading													
$[I_2(aq)]/10^{-3}$ mol dm^{-3}													

(Specimen results on page 82)

Analysis of results

1. Use your calibration curve to convert the meter readings to iodine concentrations and enter these values in Results Table 4. Calculate a value of initial concentration from the data in Table 7.

2. Plot graphs of concentration of iodine (vertical axis) against time (horizontal axis) for each mixture in the set of experiments you have done. Plot all three on the same sheet of graph paper.

3. From these graphs obtain values for the initial rate of reaction. Note that, under the conditions used in this experiment, the graphs will probably be straight lines. In this case the initial rate is simply the slope of the line. If the graphs are curves, simply draw a tangent to the curve at time zero and measure its slope.

4. Determine the order of reaction with respect to the component you have been varying, by comparing the initial rates at different concentrations.

Questions

1. Study the graphs plotted by other groups of students for varying the concentrations of the other two components. Work out the order of reaction with respect to each of these components by comparing the initial rates at different concentrations. Use all the information you have collected to write the rate equation for the reaction.

2. What is the overall order of the reaction?

3. Compare the rate equation with the stoichiometric equation for the reaction. What is the main difference between the two? How do you explain this difference?

4. Calculate the rate constant for the overall reaction using each of the three initial rates from your set of experiments and average the results. Compare this with values obtained from the other sets of experiments.

5. What are the main sources of error in this experiment?

(Answers on page 83)

Computer simulation of the experiment

If you have access to the ILPAC computer program 'Chemical Kinetics', you can use part of the program to compare your experimental results with results calculated from the accepted rate equation. Note that the other part of the program is more suitable for use later in the Unit.

The kinetics of the iodination of propanone can be investigated equally well by a sampling method such as that described in the next exercise.

Exercise 20   Under conditions of acid catalysis, propanone reacts with iodine as follows:

$$(CH_3)_2CO(aq) + I_2(aq) \rightarrow CH_2ICOCH_3(aq) + HI(aq)$$

50 cm³ of 0.02 M I_2(aq) and 50 cm³ of acidified 0.25 M propanone were mixed together. 10 cm³ portions of the reaction mixture were removed at 5 minute intervals and rapidly added to an excess of 0.5 M $NaHCO_3$(aq). The iodine remaining was titrated against aqueous sodium thiosulphate.

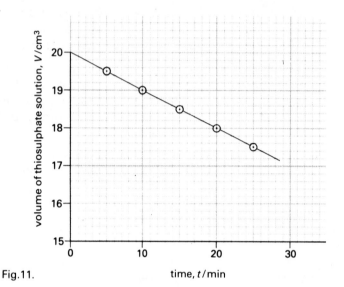

Fig.11.

The graph (Fig. 11) records the volume of aqueous sodium thiosulphate required to react with the iodine remaining at different times after mixing the reactants.

(a)   Why are the 10 cm³ portions of the reaction mixture added to aqueous sodium hydrogencarbonate before titration with sodium thiosulphate?

(b)   How does the rate of change of iodine concentration vary during the experiment?

(c)   What is the rate of reaction in terms of cm³ of sodium thiosulphate per minute?

(d)   What is the order of the reaction with respect to iodine?

(e)   Suppose the reaction is first order with respect to propanone. What would be the rate of reaction (in cm³ of sodium thiosulphate min⁻¹) if 0.50 M propanone were used instead of 0.25 M propanone?

(f)   Indicate by means of a sketch how the volume of aqueous sodium thiosulphate used would vary with time if no catalytic acid was present in the reacting mixture of propanone and iodine.

(g)   Explain your answer to (f).

(Answers on page 83)

28

Finally, in this section, we present an exercise where you are given the rate equation and the rate constant for a reaction, at a particular temperature, and asked to calculate the rates at different initial concentrations of reactants.

Exercise 21   Hydrogen and iodine react together to produce hydrogen iodide:

$$H_2(g) + I_2(g) \rightleftharpoons 2HI(g)$$

The rate equation for the reaction is:

$$\text{rate} = k\,[H_2(g)][I_2(g)]$$

and the rate constant at 374 °C is 8.58×10^{-5} mol^{-1} dm^3 s^{-1}

(a)   Work out the rate of reaction at each of the following initial concentrations of hydrogen and iodine, in experiments A, B and C.

Table 8

Expt.	Initial $[H_2]$ /mol dm^{-3}	Initial $[I_2]$ /mol dm^{-3}
A	0.010	0.050
B	0.020	0.050
C	0.020	0.10

(b)   From your answers to (a), what can you say about the effect of concentration of reactants on reaction rate?

(Answers on page 83)

COMPUTER-AIDED REVISION

At this point, if it is available, you should use the ILPAC computer program 'Chemical Kinetics'.

The program allows you to recall and practice much of what you have learned in Level One, including graphical techniques, finding orders of reaction, rate equations and rate constants. It should be good revision before you do your Level One Test. However, you should not attempt the questions about activation energy until you have done the relevant work in Level Two.

You do not need to know anything about computing but, if you have not used a program before, you will need a few minutes of instruction on getting started and using the keyboard.

LEVEL ONE CHECKLIST

You have now reached the end of Level One of this Unit. The following is a summary of the objectives in Level One. Read carefully through them and check that you have adequate notes.

At this stage you should be able to:

(1) calculate values for the rate of reaction at various times, from a graph of concentration of reactant against time;

(2) write an equation to show the relationship between rate of reaction and concentration of reactant;

(3) identify the order of reaction with respect to a named reactant;

(4) determine the overall order of reaction;

(5) work out a value for the rate constant of a first order reaction, including its units;

(6) recognise a first order reaction from a graph of rate against concentration of reactant.

(7) use a given rate equation to identify the order of reaction with respect to an individual reactant;

(8) use a given rate equation to identify the overall order of reaction;

(9) define order of reaction with respect to an individual reactant and overall order of reaction.

(10) choose suitable methods for measuring the rates of different types of reaction;

(11) describe in outline each of the main methods for measuring reaction rate.

(12) define the term half-life;

(13) determine the half-life of a first order reaction from graphical data of concentration versus time;

(14) identify a reaction with a constant half-life as being first order.

(15) determine the order of reaction with respect to individual reactants from initial rate data;

(16) determine the rate equation for the iodination of propanone by following the reactions colorimetrically.

LEVEL ONE TEST

To find out how well you have learned the material in Level One, try the test which follows. Read the notes below before starting.

1. You should spend about 1½ hours on this test.

2. You will need a sheet of graph paper and a ruler for this test.

3. Hand your answers to your teacher for marking.

LEVEL ONE TEST

In Questions 1, 2 and 3, one or more of the suggested responses is correct.
Answer as follows:

A if only 1, 2 and 3 are correct

B if only 1 and 3 are correct

C if only 2 and 4 are correct

D if only 4 is correct

E if some other response or combination is correct.

1. The extent of a reaction may be determined without interfering
    with any of the reacting materials by

    1 measuring the optical rotation

    2 measuring the electrical conductance

    3 collecting any gas evolved in a gas syringe

    4 titrating against a suitable standard solution.   (1)

2. Hydrogen peroxide oxidizes hydriodic acid according to

    $$H_2O_2(aq) + 2H^+(aq) + 2I^-(aq) \rightarrow I_2(aq) + 2H_2O(l)$$

    The rate of the reaction could be investigated by measuring
    changes in the

    1 volume of the system

    2 intensity of colour of the system

    3 optical rotation of the system

    4 electrical conductivity of the system.   (1)

3. The rate of the reaction between sodium hydroxide solution and
    ethyl propanoate

    $$C_2H_5CO_2C_2H_5(l) + OH^-(aq) \rightarrow C_2H_5CO_2^-(aq) + C_2H_5OH(aq)$$

    is first order with respect to both ethyl propanoate and sodium
    hydroxide. It is true to say that

    1 halving the concentration of either of the two reactants independ-
       ently will halve the rate of reaction

    2 the reaction is first order overall

    3 the rate of reaction is proportional to the concentration of ethyl
       propanoate

    4 halving the concentrations of both reactants simultaneously will
       halve the rate of reaction.   (1)

4. The rate of reaction between X and Y is third order overall. Which of the following rate equations must be INCORRECT?

A Rate = $k[X][Y]^3$

B Rate = $k[X][Y]^2$

C Rate = $k[X]^2[Y]$

D Rate = $k[X]^2[Y][Z]^0$

E Rate = $k[X]^0[Y]^3$

(1)

5. The rate of decomposition of a compound X in aqueous solution is given by: rate = $k[X]^2$. The units of k are

A $mol\ dm^{-3}\ s^{-1}$

B $mol^{-1}\ dm^3\ s^{-1}$

C $mol^{-1}\ dm^6\ s^{-2}$

D $mol^{-2}\ dm^6\ s^{-2}$

E $mol^{-2}\ dm^6\ s^{-1}$

(1)

6. For the reaction $X + Y \rightarrow Z$, the rate expression is

$$Rate = k[X]^2[Y]^{\frac{1}{2}}$$

If the concentrations of X and Y are both increased by a factor of 4, by what factor will the rate increase?

A 4

B 8

C 16

D 32

E 64

(1)

7. The kinetics of the reaction between MnO_4^- ions and $C_2O_4^{2-}$ ions in acidic solution is to be investigated.

$$2MnO_4^-(aq) + 16H^+(aq) + 5C_2O_4^{2-}(aq)$$
$$\rightarrow 2Mn^{2+}(aq) + 8H_2O(l) + 10CO_2(g)$$

In addition to a stop clock, which piece of apparatus would enable the rate of reaction to be followed most easily and accurately?

A Dilatometer

B Gas syringe

C Polarimeter

D Standard electrode and valve voltmeter

E Colorimeter.

(1)

8. The reaction between potassium iodide and potassium peroxodi-
    sulphate(VI), $K_2S_2O_8$, in aqueous solution proceeds according
    to the overall equation

    $$2KI(aq) + K_2S_2O_8(aq) = 2K_2SO_4(aq) + I_2$$

    The rate of this reaction is found by experiment to be directly
    proportional to the concentration of the potassium iodide, and directly
    proportional to that of the potassium peroxodisulphate(VI).

    (a) Write the above equation in ionic form.   (1)

    (b) What is the overall order of the reaction?   (1)

    (c) Show the meaning of the term velocity constant by writing an
         equation for the rate of this reaction, such that the concent-
         ration of the peroxodisulphate(VI) ions decreases with time.   (2)

    (d) With an initial concentration of potassium iodide of
         1.0×10^{-2} mol dm^{-3} and of potassium peroxodisulphate(VI) of
         5.0×10^{-4} mol dm^{-3}, it is found that at 298 K the initial rate
         of disappearance of the peroxodisulphate(VI) ions is
         1.02×10^{-8} mol dm^{-3} s^{-1}. What is the velocity constant of the
         reaction at this temperature?   (2)

9. When a dilute aqueous solution of a benzenediazonium salt is
    maintained at 35 °C, it slowly decomposes evolving nitrogen.
    The equation for the reaction is

    $$C_6H_5N_2^+(aq) + H_2O(l) \rightarrow C_6H_5OH(aq) + H^+(aq) + N_2(g)$$

    The course of the reaction may be followed by collecting the gas evolved
    and measuring its volume at known times. Three of the substances
    required for the preparation of the solution of the benzenediazonium
    salt are phenylamine, sodium nitrite and water.

    (a) Name an additional reagent which would be required for the
         preparation of the benzenediazonium salt solution.   (1)

    (b) State one condition which is necessary for the preparation of
         the benzenediazonium salt solution.   (1)

    (c) In order to follow the rate of decomposition, why is it
         necessary to stir well while the nitrogen gas is being evolved? (1)

    (d) Sketch, using the axes given below, the shape of the graph
         obtained by plotting the volume of nitrogen gas collected against
         time since the reaction began.

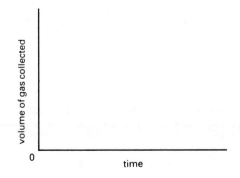

                                                                        (1)

    (e) Describe how a set of results for such an experiment, showing
         volumes of gas obtained at various times since the reaction
         began, could be used to show that the hydrolysis reaction is
         first order with respect to benzenediazonium ion.   (3)

10. In an experiment designed to investigate the effect of acid concentration on the reaction between an acid and a metal, a large excess of hydrochloric acid of concentrations varying from 0.2 M to 1.0 M reacts with a fixed length of magnesium ribbon (5 cm in each case). The reaction times required for the evolution of 15 cm³ of hydrogen gas are determined at a constant pressure of 1 atm and at 300 K.

A

The following table summarises the results obtained by a group of sixth-form students.

Concentration of hydrochloric acid /mol dm^{-3}	Time required for the evolution of 15 cm³ of hydrogen at 1 atm and 300 K/seconds
0.25	160
0.35	80
0.50	40
0.70	20
1.00	10

(a) Suggest a reason why the experiments were carried out with a large excess of hydrochloric acid. (1)

(b) Sketch out an assembly of apparatus which might have been used for carrying out the above experiments. (2)

(c) (i) Consider the data in the table. Give a relationship between reaction time t and the concentration of hydrochloric acid. (1)

   (ii) What is the order of the reaction with respect to hydrochloric acid? (1)

(d) Since hydrochloric acid is a strong acid, it contains hydrogen ions and chloride ions only. Also, as a result of this

$$[HCl] = [H^+] = [Cl^-]$$

Let n denote the overall order of the reaction between magnesium and hydrochloric acid.

Three rate equations are possible:

(i) Rate $= k[H^+]^n$

(ii) Rate $= k[H^+]^{n-p}[Cl^-]^p$

(iii) Rate $= k[Cl^-]^n$

Devise a set of investigations which would enable you to decide which one of the above rate equations is correct. (5)

34

11. Dinitrogen pentoxide (N_2O_5) decomposes according to the equation

$$2N_2O_5(g) \rightarrow 2N_2O_4(g) + O_2(g)$$

A

The reaction proceeds at a rate which is conveniently measurable at a temperature of 45 °C; at this temperature the following results were obtained.

$[N_2O_5]$/mol dm^{-3}	Rate of disappearance of N_2O_5/mol dm^{-3} s^{-1}
22.3×10^{-3}	11.65×10^{-6}
17.4×10^{-3}	8.67×10^{-6}
13.2×10^{-3}	6.63×10^{-6}
9.5×10^{-3}	4.65×10^{-6}
4.7×10^{-3}	2.35×10^{-6}

(a) Plot these results on a suitable graph. (4)

(b) The rate law for the reaction can be expressed in the form

$$\text{rate} = k[N_2O_5]^x$$

   (i) What is the value of x as deduced from the graph? (1)

   (ii) What is the value of k at 45 °C? In what units is it expressed? (2)

(c) It can be calculated from the figures given that the concentration would fall from 2×10^{-2} mol dm^{-3} to 1×10^{-2} mol dm^3 in 1386 seconds. How much longer would it take to fall to 2.5×10^{-3} mol dm^{-3}? (2)

(d) It will be seen from the equation that two N_2O_5 molecules give rise to three molecules of products. (You may neglect dissociation of N_2O_4 at this temperature.)

   (i) Indicate how in principle you would use this fact to follow the extent of decomposition of N_2O_5 with time. (2)

   (ii) Sketch a simple apparatus that could be used for this purpose. (2)

(Continued on page 36.)

12. The table shows the results of an investigation into the rate of reaction between hydroxide ions, OH^-, and phosphinate ions, $PH_2O_2^-$, at 80 °C. The overall equation for the reaction is:

$$PH_2O_2^-(aq) + OH^-(aq) \rightarrow PHO_3^{2-}(aq) + H_2(g)$$

Experiment	Initial concentrations		Initial rate of hydrogen production /cm³ min⁻¹
	$[PH_2O_2^-(aq)]$ /mol dm⁻³	$[OH^-(aq)]$ /mol dm⁻³	
1	0.6	1.0	2.4
2	0.6	2.0	9.6
3	0.6	3.0	21.5
4	0.1	6.0	14.4
5	0.2	6.0	28.8
6	0.3	6.0	43.2

(a) How does the initial rate of this reaction depend on the concentration of hydroxide ions? (1)

(b) How does the initial rate of this reaction depend on the concentration of phosphinate ions? (1)

(c) What is the rate expression for this reaction? (2)

(d) In what units will the rate constant be expressed? (1)

(e) Is the hydroxide ion acting as a base in this reaction? Justify your answer. (2)

(Total 50 marks)

LEVEL TWO

In the next section we show how the rate equation for a chemical reaction can be used to work out a possible mechanism. Proposing a mechanism involves suggesting, at a molecular level, the route by which the reaction occurs.

REACTION MECHANISMS

Objectives. When you have finished this section you should be able to:

(17) explain why a reaction mechanism can be worked out only from the rate equation for a reaction, not directly from the stoichiometric equation;

(18) state that most chemical reactions take place in a series of steps, each called an elementary step or reaction step;

(19) explain the meaning of the term molecularity;

(20) distinguish between the molecularity of a reaction step and the order of reaction as shown by the rate equation;

(21) identify the slowest step in a reaction as the rate-determining step;

(22) suggest a simple mechanism for a reaction from the rate equation and vice versa.

Molecularity

Start by reading about molecularity and rate-determining step in your text book(s). Look in the index under 'reaction mechanism' or 'mechanism of a reaction'. Make sure that you understand the difference between molecularity and order of reaction and that the term molecularity can strictly be applied only to a reaction step and not to the overall reaction.

A reaction with more than three reacting species is unlikely to take place in a single step. The probability of even three particles colliding and reacting instantaneously is very small. We assume that most of these reactions which proceed at a measurable rate occur in two or more separate steps. The series of reaction steps, taken together, is the reaction mechanism, or reaction pathway as it is sometimes called.

In the next exercise you consider the mechanism for the iodine-propanone reaction whose rate equation you have determined experimentally and found to be: Rate = $k[CH_3COCH_3][H^+]$

Exercise 22   A suggested mechanism for the iodination of propanone is:
is:

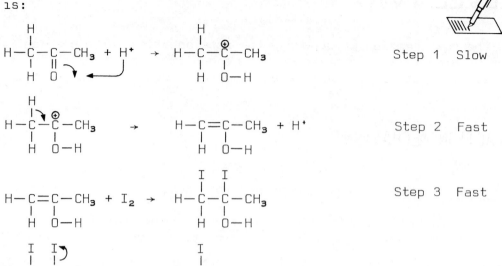

Step 1   Slow

Step 2   Fast

Step 3   Fast

Step 4   Fast

(a)   Write down the molecularity of each step.

(b)   Does the mechanism show H^+(aq) acting as a catalyst?

(Answers on page 84)

Notice that in the above mechanism the first step is slow whilst the others
are fast. This slow step is called the rate-determining step and
information concerning it is obtained from the rate equation.

The rate-determining step

Whenever a process takes place in several steps, the overall rate of the
process depends on the speed of the slowest step. There are lots of
situations like this; for example, driving along a busy motorway which
converges into a single lane and then opens up again into three lanes.
Consider Fig. 12 below and imagine you want to travel from A to D.

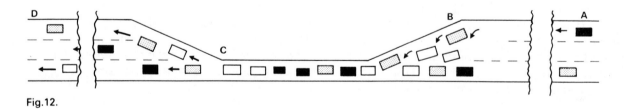

Fig.12.

If at A your car is travelling at 70 m.p.h. you will reach point B quickly
but getting past the lane closure can take a long time. Once your car has
reached C it can accelerate again and arrive at D shortly afterwards. In this
analogy the stages correspond to the elementary steps in a reaction mechanism.

In a more realistic comparison with a three-step chemical reaction your
speed from A to B would be so great that the distance A - B is immaterial,
and it would take several days to get past the lane closure. Thus, getting
past the lane closure is the rate-determining step, i.e. it determines the
overall rate of travel from A to D.

38

You may disagree with this analogy. It may not represent all the steps; it can only be suggested, then tested. The same is true for mechanisms of chemical reactions. Keep thinking about the idea of rate-determining steps in odd moments over the next few days. Can you suggest a better analogy than the one we describe above?

Now we look at the ways in which we decide what might be the rate-determining step in a chemical reaction.

Proposing a reaction mechanism

In any reaction mechanism of the type that you are likely to meet, there is usually one step which acts as a bottleneck, the rate-determining step for the reaction. The only way to find out which molecules and how many of them are involved in the rate-determining step is to look at the rate equation for the reaction.

We now take you through a Worked Example to show you how to identify the rate-determining step and to suggest a mechanism for a reaction.

Worked Example. Hydrogen and iodine monochloride react as shown by the equation:

$$2ICl(g) + H_2(g) \rightarrow 2HCl(g) + I_2(g)$$

The rate equation for the reaction is:

$$rate = k[ICl(g)][H_2(g)]$$

Suggest a possible mechanism for the reaction.

Solution

1. Decide which molecules (species) are involved in the rate-determining step:

   The rate equation shows that the reaction is of the first order with respect to ICl and first order with respect to H_2. The rate-determining step is likely to involve ICl and H_2 in a collision.

   $$ICl(g) + H_2(g) \rightarrow products$$

2. Suggest possible products from the reactants you have chosen:

   (These products may include species which do not appear as products in the stoichiometric equation.)
   The most probable products for the reaction between ICl and H_2 are HCl and HI. Thus we can write the equation for the rate-determining step:

   $$ICl(g) + H_2(g) \rightarrow HCl(g) + HI(g) \quad SLOW$$

3. Compare the rate-determining step with the stoichiometric equation to see how many molecules are still to be accounted for:

   We have to account for another molecule of ICl. HI is not a final product so a second step might be:

   $$ICl(g) + HI(g) \rightarrow HCl(g) + I_2(g) \quad FAST$$

4.   Add up the reaction steps:

Intermediate products and reactants should cancel, so that the steps, taken together, contain the same amounts of reactants and products given in the stoichiometric equation. If they do not add up to the stoichiometric equation your mechanism can't possibly work!

Adding up the steps for this reaction, we have:

$$ICl(g) + H_2(g) \rightarrow HCl(g) + HI(g) \qquad \text{slow}$$
$$ICl(g) + HI(g) \rightarrow HCl(g) + I_2(g) \qquad \text{fast}$$
$$\overline{2ICl(g) + H_2(g) \rightarrow 2HCl(g) + I_2(g)} \qquad \text{(overall reaction)}$$

The separate steps do add up to give the same overall amounts of reactants and products as the stoichiometric equation, and so this is a possible mechanism. It must be accepted as a possibility unless and until it is disproved as the result of further experimental work. For example, if the reaction mixture were shown to contain traces of chlorine, the above mechanism would not fit all the facts and a new one would have to be found.

Now try the next exercise, where we give alternative mechanisms for the above reaction.

Exercise 23   The following mechanisms have been proposed for the reaction between iodine monochloride and hydrogen, but none of them is satisfactory. Identify the main fault(s) in each mechanism. Assume all species are gaseous.

(a) $ICl + H_2 \rightarrow HCl + HI \qquad \text{slow}$

$HCl + ICl \rightarrow HI + Cl_2 \qquad \text{fast}$

$Cl_2 + HI \rightarrow HCl + ICl \qquad \text{fast}$

(b) $ICl + ICl \rightarrow I_2 + Cl_2 \qquad \text{slow}$

$Cl_2 + H_2 \rightarrow 2HCl \qquad \text{fast}$

(c) $ICl \rightarrow I\cdot + Cl\cdot \qquad \text{slow}$

$I\cdot + H_2 \rightarrow HI + H\cdot \qquad \text{fast}$

$H\cdot + ICl \rightarrow HI + Cl\cdot \qquad \text{fast}$

$Cl\cdot + Cl\cdot \rightarrow Cl_2 \qquad \text{fast}$

$HI + HI \rightarrow I_2 + H_2 \qquad \text{fast}$

$Cl_2 + H_2 \rightarrow 2HCl \qquad \text{fast}$

(Answers on page 84)

In the next exercise you refer back to the proposed mechanism for the iodination of propanone which appeared in Exercise 22.

40

Exercise 24   Study the mechanism for the iodination of propanone
given in Exercise 22 (page 38) and answer the following
questions.

(a)   Identify the rate-determining step.

(b)   What is the relationship between the molecularity of the
rate-determining step and the rate equation?

(c)   Add up the reaction steps and show that the overall
reaction agrees with the stoichiometric equation.

(Answers on page 84)

In Exercises 16, 18 and 19 in Level One, which were part A-level questions,
you worked out rate equations for three reactions from data. We now add
another part of each question, which asks you to suggest a mechanism for
each reaction.

Exercise 25   Given that the reaction: $2N_2O_5 \rightarrow 4NO_2 + O_2$

is first order, suggest a mechanism to account for this.

(Answer on page 84)

Exercise 26   For the reaction: $A + 3B \rightarrow AB_3$

the rate equation is: rate = $k[A][B]^2$

Suggest a possible mechanism for the reaction between
A and B, leading to the formation of AB_3.

(Answer on page 84)

Exercise 27   For the reaction $2H_2(g) + 2NO(g) \rightarrow 2H_2O(g) + N_2(g)$

the rate equation is: rate = $k[H_2][NO]^2$

Suggest a possible mechanism which is consistent with
the rate equation.

(Answer on page 84)

Now that you have had some practice in working out mechanisms for reactions,
we go on to consider one example in more detail, the hydrolysis of halogenoalkanes.

The hydrolysis of halogenoalkanes

You have already studied the hydrolysis of primary, secondary and tertiary halogenoalkanes in Unit 02 (Some Functional Groups) and considered the mechanism for the hydrolysis of a primary halogenoalkane.

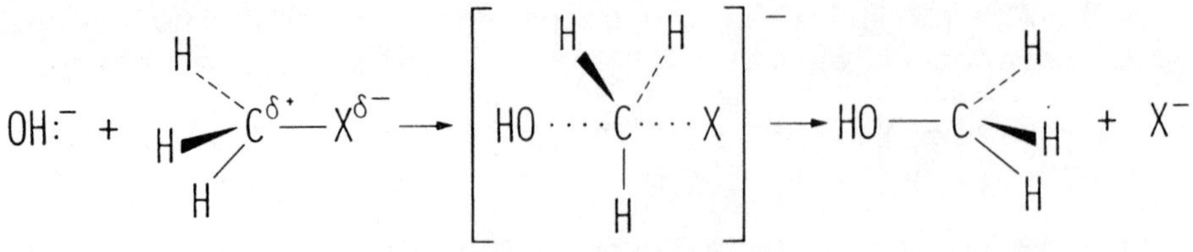

Fig.13.   activated complex

We study this mechanism in the light of its rate equation and consider the mechanisms for the hydrolyses of secondary and tertiary halogenoalkanes.

Objectives. When you have finished this section you should be able to:

(23) use the rate equation for the hydrolysis of a halogenoalkane to work out a mechanism for the reaction;

(24) explain the effect of the carbon skeleton on the rate of hydrolysis of halogenoalkanes in terms of the stability of carbonium ions.

Many experiments have been carried out to investigate the hydrolysis reactions of halogenoalkanes. In the next exercise we present initial-rate data from a series of experiments carried out on bromomethane and 2-bromo-2-methylpropane. Use the data to work out the rate equation for the hydrolysis of each compound.

Exercise 28   Samples of bromomethane and 2-bromo-2-methylpropane were dissolved in dilute aqueous ethanol and reacted with sodium hydroxide solution. Several experiments were carried out, at constant temperature, using different initial concentrations of each bromoalkane and hydroxide ions. The initial rate of reaction was determined in each case. Use the data to establish a rate equation for each reaction.

Table 9   Data for the hydrolysis of bromomethane, CH_3Br

Experiment	$[CH_3Br]$ /mol dm^{-3}	$[OH^-]$ /mol dm^{-3}	Rate /mol dm^{-3} s^{-1}
A	0.010	0.0050	0.107
B	0.010	0.010	0.216
C	0.010	0.020	0.425
D	0.020	0.020	0.856
E	0.040	0.020	1.72
F	0.080	0.020	3.42

Table 10   Data for the hydrolysis of 2-bromo-2-methylpropane, $(CH_3)_3CBr$

Experiment	$[(CH_3)_3CBr]$ /mol dm^{-3}	$[OH^-]$ /mol dm^{-3}	Rate /mol dm^{-3} s^{-1}
A	0.020	0.010	20.2
B	0.020	0.020	20.1
C	0.020	0.030	20.2
D	0.040	0.030	40.1
E	0.060	0.030	60.2
F	0.080	0.030	80.0

(a) Use the data to establish a rate equation for each reaction.

(b) Identify the rate-determining step in the mechanism for the hydrolysis of bromomethane shown in Fig.13 .

(c) Propose a mechanism for the hydrolysis of 2-bromo-2-methylpropane. (Hint: the mechanism involves the formation of a carbonium ion.)

(d) Why do you think the mechanism for the primary halogeno-alkane is labelled S$_N$2 and the mechanism for the tertiary halogenoalkane is labelled S$_N$1?

(Answers on page 84)

You should now make a space-filling model of the tertiary halide and use it to do the next short exercise.

Exercise 29   What feature of the structure of $(CH_3)_3CBr$ makes a bimolecular mechanism for its hydrolysis unlikely?

(Answer on page 84)

In Unit 01 (Hydrocarbons) you learned that tertiary carbonium ions are more stable than primary carbonium ions. We can therefore conclude that tertiary halogenoalkanes hydrolyse via the S$_N$1 mechanism partly because of the steric problems associated with the 'activated complex' and partly due to the greater stability of the tertiary carbonium ion compared to that of the primary carbonium ion.

The kinetics of hydrolysis of secondary halogenoalkanes are intermediate between those for primary and tertiary halogenoalkanes. The rate equation is more complex than the examples you have met so far and you are not expected to know it for most A-level syllabuses. We give it below for completeness and draw certain conclusions from it.

$$Rate = k_1[RX] + k_2[RX][OH^-]$$

where RX is the halogenoalkane. The relative importance of the two terms $k_1[RX]$ and $k_2[RX][OH^-]$ depends on the reaction conditions and the structure of the halogenoalkane. Thus secondary halides may react according to either S$_N$1 or S$_N$2 mechanisms depending on the conditions.

If it is available, you should now watch part 2 of the ILPAC video-programme 'Chemical Kinetics' which deals with mechanisms, including those of the halogenoalkane hydrolyses.

The next exercise is an A-level question based on a different reaction. You are given data and asked to use these to determine the order of reaction and comment on its mechanism.

Exercise 30   In the Journal of the Chemical Society for 1950, Hughes, Ingold and Reed report some kinetic studies on aromatic nitration. In one experiment ethanoic acid containing 0.2% water was used as solvent and pure nitric acid was added to make a 7 M solution.

The kinetics of the nitration of ethylbenzene, $C_6H_5C_2H_5$, were studied with the following results at 20 °C.

Table 11

Time /min	Concentration of ethylbenzene/mol dm^{-3}
0	0.090
8.0	0.063
11.0	0.053
13.0	0.049
16.0	0.037
21.0	0.024
25.0	0.009

(a) Determine an order of reaction from these results.

(b) What does this suggest about the mechanism of the reaction?

(c) What products are likely?

(Answers on page 85)

We now go on to consider the effect of temperature on the rate of reaction, and introduce the important concept of activation energy.

ACTIVATION ENERGY AND THE EFFECT OF TEMPERATURE ON REACTION RATE

The rate of many gaseous and aqueous reactions often doubles for a temperature rise of only 10 K. Why is it that such a small rise in temperature can cause a large percentage increase in the reaction rate? We consider the question in the following section, which also helps to explain why some reactions, which we might expect to proceed on the basis of values of $\Delta H^{\ominus}$ or $\Delta G^{\ominus}$, do not appear to occur.

<u>Objectives.</u> When you have finished this section you should be able to:

(25) state the meaning of the term <u>activation energy</u> and identify it on an energy profile diagram for a reaction;

(26) explain the <u>effect of increased temperature</u> on the rate of reaction in terms of the <u>fraction of molecules with energy greater than the activation energy;</u>

(27) state the <u>Arrhenius equation,</u>which shows how the rate constant, k, changes with temperature;

(28) use a graphical method to obtain values for the <u>activation energy</u> from the <u>Arrhenius equation.</u>

Read the section on activation energy in your text-book(s). Look for energy profile diagrams indicating activation energy. This will help you to answer the exercises which follow.

Consider the following reaction:

$$C_8H_{18}(l) + 12\tfrac{1}{2}O_2(g) \rightarrow 8CO_2(g) + 9H_2O(g); \quad \Delta H = -5498 \text{ kJ mol}^{-1}$$

This reaction is highly exothermic and can occur with explosive force under the right conditions. However, it does not take place at room temperature!

There are many other examples like this, where there is an 'energy barrier' to be overcome before reaction can take place. This barrier is called the activation energy for the reaction. Since collisions between reactant particles are always occurring it seems reasonable to assume that particles do not always react when they collide. A reaction occurs as a result of collisions between particles which possess more than a certain minimum amount of energy - the activation energy, E_a (sometimes E_A).

The next exercise is concerned with the energy barrier and the forces which need to be overcome before a reaction can occur.

<u>Exercise 31</u> Suggest two reasons why molecules must reach a certain energy before reaction between them is possible.

(Answers on page 85)

An energy profile diagram is a way of showing how the energy of reacting molecules changes. To ensure that you can distinguish between the activation energy and the enthalpy change for a reaction, try the next exercise.

<u>Exercise 32</u> (a) Draw an energy profile to represent the reaction:

$$2N_2O(g) \rightleftharpoons 2N_2(g) + O_2(g); \quad \Delta H^{\ominus} = -164.0 \text{ kJ mol}^{-1}$$

The activation energy, E_a, for the forward reaction is 250 kJ mol^{-1}. Use graph paper and let 1 cm represent 50 kJ mol^{-1}.

(b) Use your energy profile diagram to calculate the activation energy for the back reaction.

(Answers on page 85)

Next we go on to consider what proportion of particles in a gaseous reaction mixture reach the activation energy and how the proportion is affected by temperature.

The fraction of particles with energy greater than E_a

In Unit P1 (The Gaseous State) you learned about the Maxwell distribution curves for a sample of gas at different temperatures. You then used these curves to calculate the fraction of molecules with kinetic energies in a certain range at a particular temperature. For our purposes, in this Unit, it would be useful to know the fraction of molecules with energy greater than the energy of activation, E_a.

Consider Fig. 14 below, which shows the distribution of kinetic energies of particles in the gas phase and the activation energy, E_a.

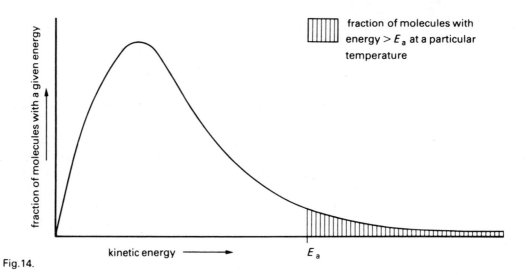

Fig.14.

The area beneath the curve is proportional to the total number of particles involved and the shaded area under the curve is proportional to the number of particles with energy greater than E_a. Hence the fraction of particles with energy greater than E_a is given by the ratio:

$$\frac{\text{shaded area under curve}}{\text{total area under curve}} = \frac{\text{number of particles with } E > E_a}{\text{total number of particles}}$$

Maxwell and Boltzmann derived a useful mathematical expression for this fraction in terms of the activation energy, E_a, the gas constant, R, and the absolute temperature, T:

$$\boxed{\text{Fraction of particles with energy} > E_a = e^{-E_a/RT}}$$

The following Worked Example shows you how to use this expression to calculate the number of molecules with energy greater than a given energy.

<u>Worked Example.</u> Calculate the number of molecules in 1.0 mol of gas at 25 °C with energy greater than 55.0 kJ mol⁻¹.

46

Solution

1. Calculate the fraction of molecules with energy greater than
    55.0 kJ mol^{-1}.

    Fraction of molecules with $E > 55.0$ kJ mol^{-1} = $e^{-E/RT}$ where
    $R = 8.31$ J K^{-1} mol, $T = 298$ K and $E = 55000$ J mol^{-1}.

    $\therefore$ Fraction of molecules = $e^{-(55000 \text{ J mol}^{-1})/(8.31 \text{ J K}^{-1} \text{ mol}^{-1})(298 \text{ K})}$

    $= e^{-22.2}$ $= 2.28 \times 10^{-10}$

2. Calculate the total number of molecules with energy greater than
    55.0 kJ mol^{-1}.

    The total number of molecules present in 1.0 mol of gas is given by:

    $L = 6.02 \times 10^{23}$ mol^{-1} where L is the Avogadro constant.

    Since fraction of molecules with $E > 55.0$ kJ mol^{-1} = $\dfrac{\text{number of molecules with } E > 55.0 \text{ kJ mol}^{-1}}{\text{total number of molecules}}$

    Then number with $E > 55.0$ kJ mol^{-1} = $L\, e^{-E/RT}$

    $= 6.02 \times 10^{23}$ mol^{-1} $\times 2.28 \times 10^{-10}$ = $\boxed{1.37 \times 10^{14} \text{ mol}^{-1}}$

Now you do a similar calculation at a different temperature.

Exercise 33 (a) Calculate the number of molecules in 1.0 mol of gas
                  at 35 °C with energy greater than 55.0 kJ mol^{-1}.

             (b) Compare this value to that worked out at 298 K.

             (Answers on page 85)

You have just calculated that for a rise in temperature of only 10 K twice
as many molecules exceed the energy barrier of 55.0 kJ mol^{-1}. Thus, on the
Maxwell distribution curves the shaded area under the $(T + 10)$ K curve will
be twice that on the T K curve (where T is the absolute temperature) as
shown in Fig. 15.

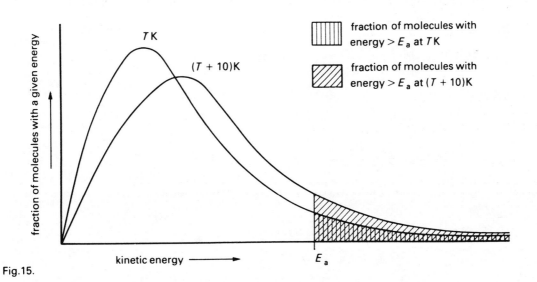

Fig.15.

We now go on to consider the relationship between the rate constant, k, for
a reaction and the fraction of particles with energy greater than E_a.

THE ARRHENIUS EQUATION

For particles to react, their energy must exceed E_a for that reaction. This suggests that at a given temperature

$$\text{Rate} \propto e^{-E_a/RT} \dots\dots\dots\dots(1)$$

Since the rate changes during the progress of a reaction, it is more useful to use k (rate constant).

Consider the general reaction

$$A(g) + B(g) \rightarrow \text{products}$$

$$\text{Rate} = k[A]^x[B]^y \text{ at a room temperature } T_1$$

If the experiment is repeated using the same concentrations of A and B at a higher temperature, T_2, the rate increases. Since $[A]^x$ and $[B]^x$ have the same initial value then k must increase. Therefore, we can say that the rate constant is a general measure of the reaction rate at a particular temperature. Equation (1) becomes:

$$k \propto e^{-E_a/RT}$$

$$\therefore \quad k = Ae^{-E_a/RT} \dots\dots\dots\dots\dots(2)$$

A is a constant, sometimes called the Arrhenius constant or pre-exponential constant. Equation (2) is often called the Arrhenius equation, named after the Swedish chemist, Svante Arrhenius, who formulated it in 1880.

Fig.16. S.A. Arrhenius (1859-1927)

Using the Arrhenius equation

The equation provides an extremely useful means of getting values for the activation energy and the pre-exponential factor for a reaction. It is usually changed to a logarithmic form to make it more manageable:

$$k = Ae^{-E_a/RT}$$

$$\therefore \quad \ln k = \ln Ae^{-E_a/RT} \qquad (\ln = \log_e)$$

$$= \ln A + \ln e^{-E_a/RT}$$

$$= \ln A - E_a/RT$$

Changing this to the $\log_{10}$ form:

$$\log_{10}k = \log_{10}A - \frac{E_a}{2.3\ RT}\dots\dots\dots\dots(3)$$

Equation (3) is often quoted for you in A-level questions.

The next exercise deals with equation (3).

Exercise 34   (a)   Which of the terms in equation (3) are variables
                    for a particular reaction?

            (b)   Compare equation (3) to the equation for a straight
                    line, i.e. $y = mx + c$. Which of the terms in
                    equation (3) are analogous to y, m, x and c?

            (c)   Sketch the shape of the graph you would expect to obtain
                    by plotting $\log_{10} k$ against $1/T$.

            (d)   Show how you could calculate A and E_a from your graph.

            (Answers on page 85)

Use the method you have just devised in the next exercise.

Exercise 35   When gaseous hydrogen iodide decomposes in accordance
            with the equation:

                 $2HI(g) \rightleftharpoons H_2(g) + I_2(g)$

            the reaction is found to be second order with respect to
            hydrogen iodide. In a series of experiments, the rate constant
            for this reaction was determined at several different tempe-
            ratures. The results obtained are shown in the table below.

Table 12

Temperature (T)/K	Rate constant (k) /dm³ mol⁻¹ s⁻¹
633	1.78×10^{-5}
666	1.07×10^{-4}
697	5.01×10^{-4}
715	1.05×10^{-3}
781	1.51×10^{-2}

Arrhenius deduced that for a reaction:

$$\log k = \frac{-E}{2.3\,RT} + \log A$$

where R is the gas constant and A is a constant.

(a)   Use the data given to determine the activation energy E
        for the reaction.

(b)   Determine by what factor the rate increases when the
        temperature rises from 300 K to 310 K.
        (You may wish to use the alternative form of the Arrhenius
        equation

             $k = A\ 10^{-E/2.3RT}$)

(c)   The kinetic energy of a fixed mass of gas is directly
        proportional to its temperature measured on the Kelvin
        scale. Calculate the ratio of the kinetic energies of a
        fixed mass of gas at 310 K and at 300 K.

(d)   Compare this ratio with the increase in the rate of
        reaction determined from experimental data. Discuss the
        significance of this result.

(Answers on page 86)

In the next experiment you determine the activation energy for the oxidation of iodide ions by peroxodisulphate(VI) (persulphate) ions. The experiment is an example of a 'clock' reaction, in which you measure the time taken for a reaction to reach a certain stage. You will find more details on 'clock' reactions in Appendix Two of this Unit.

EXPERIMENT 3
Determining the activation energy of a reaction

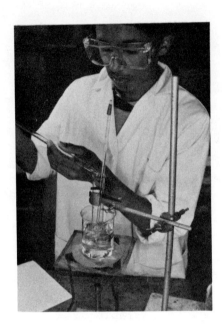

Aim

The purpose of this experiment is to determine the activation energy, E_a, for the reduction of peroxodisulphate(VI) ions, $S_2O_8{}^{2-}$(aq), by iodide ions, I^-(aq), using a 'clock' reaction.

Introduction

The equation for the reduction of peroxodisulphate(VI) ions by iodide ions is:

$$S_2O_8{}^{2-}(aq) + 2I^-(aq) \rightarrow 2SO_4{}^{2-}(aq) + I_2(aq)$$

A small, known amount of thiosulphate ions is added to the reaction mixture, which also contains some starch indicator. The thiosulphate reacts with the iodine formed in the above reaction as in the following equation:

$$2S_2O_3{}^{2-}(aq) + I_2(aq) \rightarrow S_4O_6{}^{2-}(aq) + 2I^-(aq)$$

At the instant that all the thiosulphate has reacted, free iodine is produced in the solution and its presence is shown by the appearance of the blue-black colour of the iodine-starch complex, i.e. the thiosulphate ions act as a 'monitor' indicating the point at which a certain amount of iodine has been formed. For this reason the reaction is often referred to as an iodine 'clock' reaction. In general, for a 'clock' reaction:

Rate of reaction $\propto 1/t$ where t is the time taken to reach a specified stage.

You carry out the experiment at five different temperatures between about 20 °C and 50 °C. You then find the activation energy for the reaction by plotting a graph of log $(1/t)$ against $1/T$ (T is the absolute temperature)

Requirements

safety spectacles
beaker, 400 cm^3
2 thermometers, 0-100 °C
Bunsen burner, tripod, gauze and mat
4 burettes and stands, with beakers and funnels for filling
2 boiling-tubes
clamp and stand
potassium peroxodisulphate(VI) solution, 0.020 M $K_2S_2O_8$
potassium iodide solution, 0.50 M KI
sodium thiosulphate solution, 0.010 M $Na_2S_2O_3$
starch solution, 0.2%
stopclock or watch

50

Procedure

1. Half-fill the beaker with water and heat it to between 49 °C and 51 °C. This will be used as a water-bath.

2. Using a burette, measure out 10 cm³ of potassium peroxodisulphate(VI) solution into the first boiling-tube. Clamp this in the water-bath and place a thermometer in the solution in the boiling-tube.

3. Using burettes, measure out 5 cm³ each of the potassium iodide and sodium thiosulphate solutions and 2.5 cm³ of starch solution into the second boiling-tube. Place another thermometer in this solution and stand it in the water-bath.

4. When the temperatures of the two solutions are equal and constant (to within ± 1 °C), pour the contents of the second boiling-tube into the first, shake to mix, and start the clock.

5. When the blue colour of the starch-iodine complex appears, stop the clock and write down the time in a copy of Results Table 5.

6. Repeat the experiment at temperatures close to 45 °C, 40 °C, 35 °C, 30 °C. (The temperatures you use may differ from those by a few degrees but must, of course, be recorded carefully.)

Results Table 5

Temperature/°C					
Temperature, T/K					
Time, t/s					
$\log_{10}(1/t)$					
$\frac{1}{T}$/K^{-1}					

(Specimen results on page **86**)

Calculations

1. Plot a graph of $\log_{10}(1/t)$ (vertical axis) against $1/T$ (horizontal axis).

2. Use your graph to calculate a value for the activation energy.

(Answers on page **86**)

The experiment you have just performed can be automated using a micro-computer (see Fig. 17). Ask your teacher for details, if you are interested in finding out how this is done.

Fig.17.

In the next exercise we present data for a reaction between peroxo-
disulphate(VI) ions and cobalt metal. In this case, you take the units of
k as loss in mass of metal per minute and work out a value for the activation
energy for the reaction.

Exercise 36   When strips of cobalt foil are rotated rapidly at a
               constant rate in sodium peroxodisulphate(VI) solution,
               there is a slow reaction and the cobalt dissolves. The
               reaction can be followed by removing and weighing the
               foil at intervals.

Table 13

Experiment 1 at 0.5 °C		Experiment 2 at 13.5 °C		Experiment 3 at 25 °C	
Time /min	Mass /mg	Time /min	Mass /mg	Time /min	Mass /mg
0	130	0	130	0	130
20	120	10	115	4	116
60	98	15	106	8	103
80	86	30	86	12	87

Determine a rate constant k at each temperature as a loss in
mass per minute (mg min^{-1}), and then determine the activation
energy E of the reaction using the relationship

$$k \propto 10^{-E/2.3RT}$$

What difference in the results would you predict if the cobalt
foil were NOT rotated?

(Answers on page 87)

The ILPAC computer program 'Chemical Kinetics' contains a section on
activation energy. If it is available, and if you have time, you
could now run this part of the program in order to test your understanding of the topic. Ask your teacher.

We turn now to another factor affecting the rate of chemical reactions, the
presence of catalysts.

CATALYSIS

A catalyst can be defined as a substance which alters the rate of a reaction
without itself undergoing any permanent chemical change. In this section
we consider the effect of a catalyst on the activation energy of the
reaction and the mechanism of catalysis.

<u>Objectives.</u> When you have finished this section you should be able to:

(29) describe the difference between <u>homogeneous</u> and <u>heterogeneous</u>
      <u>catalysis</u> and give examples of each type;

(30) explain the action of a <u>catalyst</u> in terms of <u>activation energy</u> and
      <u>reaction pathways</u>;

(31) explain what happens in an <u>autocatalytic reaction</u> and give one example
      of this type of reaction.

Start by reading the section on catalysis in your text-book(s). At
this stage, read rapidly through the whole section, keeping the above
objectives in mind as a guide. You will need to read some parts in
more detail later.

You have already met several reactions which are catalysed. In the
next exercise you recall some examples of catalysed reactions and classify
the catalysts involved as homogeneous or heterogeneous. If the reactants
are in a different physical state from the catalyst then the catalyst is
classed as a heterogeneous catalyst. If the reactants and catalyst are in
the same physical state then it is classed as a homogeneous catalyst. Use
this information to answer the following question.

<u>Exercise 37</u>   Choose six reactions that you have studied so far in
             your course which are catalysed. Write your answer in
             the form of a table with three columns, classifying your
             catalyst as homogeneous or heterogeneous in the third
             column.

             (Answers on page 87)

In the iodination of propanone you learned that the H⁺ ions which catalyse
the reaction do not appear as reactants in the stoichiometric equation but
they do appear in the rate equation. This is generally the case if the
catalyst is involved in the rate-determining step of the reaction. However,
catalysts are not always involved in the rate-determining step and in such
cases do not usually appear as concentration terms in the rate equation.

In the next section, we consider the way in which a catalyst can affect the
rate of reaction without necessarily being involved in the rate-determining
step.

Catalysts and activation energy

Most catalysts are thought to operate by providing an alternative reaction
pathway with a lower activation energy. The catalysed reaction proceeds by
a different mechanism, which may involve more reaction steps than the
uncatalysed one, but it takes place more rapidly because each step has a lower
activation energy than that of the uncatalysed reaction.

It's a bit like crossing the Alps from Italy to France. One way is on foot
- climbing up glaciers with ropes and crampons, and this requires a huge
amount of energy. This is the uncatalysed route. The other way is to go
under Mont Blanc in your car, using the road tunnel - a different route,
which is faster.

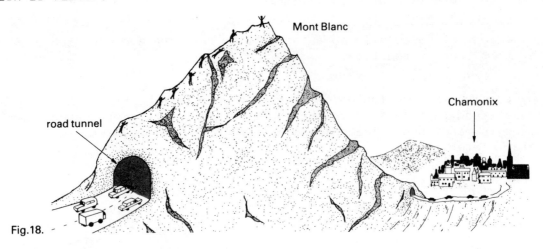

Fig.18.

In the next exercise, you interpret an energy profile diagram for the decomposition of hydrogen iodide, both catalysed and uncatalysed.

Exercise 38   The decomposition of hydrogen iodide is catalysed by
               platinum metal. The following diagram, Fig.19,
               represents the energy changes that take place during the
               course of the uncatalysed reaction, with the changes
               during the catalysed reaction superimposed.

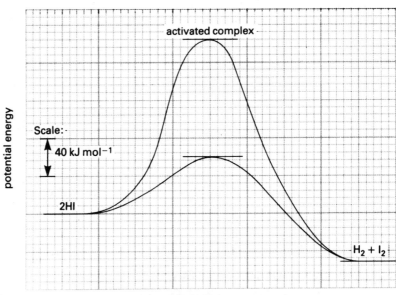

Fig.19.   progress of reaction →

Use the scale on Fig. 19 to work out the following for both the
forward and back reactions:

(a) the activation energies (uncatalysed),

(b) the activation energies (catalysed),

(c) the enthalpy changes.

(Answers on page 87)

The energy profile (Fig. 19) shows that, by lowering the activation energy, the catalyst speeds up both the forward and back reactions.

We consider more fully the mechanism of catalysis in Unit I5 (Transition Elements). However, before ending this section, we take a brief look at reactions where the catalyst is also a product of the reaction.

Autocatalysis

Reactions in which a product acts as a catalyst are called 'autocatalytic'. Once the reaction starts, more catalyst is produced, so that the rate of reaction <u>increases</u> with time for at least part of its duration. You have already come across one example of a reaction like this in Level One - the acid-catalysed iodination of propanone:

$$CH_3COCH_3(aq) + I_2(aq) \rightarrow CH_2ICOCH_3(aq) + H^+(aq) + I^-(aq)$$

The ILPAC computer program 'Chemical Kinetics' has a section which illustrates the autocatalytic nature of this reaction. Ask your teacher if it is available.

C

The next exercise is about the autocatalytic oxidation of manganate(VII) ions, MnO_4^-, by ethanedioate ions, $C_2O_4^{2-}$, catalysed by manganese(II) ions, Mn^{2+}.

$$2MnO_4^-(aq) + 16H^+(aq) + 2C_2O_4^{2-}(aq) \rightarrow 4CO_2(g) + 2Mn^{2+}(aq) + 8H_2O(l)$$

<u>Exercise 39</u>   The graph in Fig. 20 represents the reaction between manganate(VII) ions and ethanedioate ions.

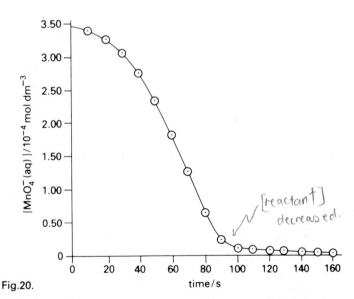

Fig.20.

(a)   Estimate from the graph the rates of reaction at the beginning of the process and after 50 seconds. How do you explain the difference in these values?

(b)   The rate of reaction suddenly drops again after about 90 seconds. Give a reason for this.

(Answers on page 87)

55

In the next experiment, which you are expected to plan in advance, you determine the activation energy for the catalysed reaction you studied in Experiment 3. If you have studied Unit I5 you will have discovered that this experiment is catalysed by iron(III) ions, which you use in this experiment.

EXPERIMENT 4
Determining the activation energy of a catalysed reaction

Aim

The purpose of this experiment is to determine the activation energy for the oxidation of iodide ions by peroxo-disulphate(VI) ions in the presence of iron(III) ions. You then compare the value obtained with that for the uncatalysed reaction, determined in Experiment 3.

Introduction

Because this is a planning experiment, we give fewer details and instructions than you have been used to. It is, of course, very similar to Experiment 3 but you should consider carefully which concentrations of solutions to use since the reaction is catalysed. You should also consider the effect of temperature on reaction rate.

Requirements

Make a list of requirements including the masses and amounts needed: discuss the list with your teacher or technician at least a day before you want to do the experiment.

Procedure

Work this out for yourself and keep an accurate record.

Results

1. Tabulate your results in an appropriate form.

2. Calculate a value for the activation energy of this reaction.

(Your teacher has a set of specimen results)

Question

Compare your result with the activation energy you calculated in Experiment 3. Comment on the two values, and discuss them with your teacher.

You should now attempt the following Teacher-marked Exercise which is concerned with activation energy and catalysis.

When ethanal is heated to about 800 K, it decomposes by a second order reaction according to the equation

$$CH_3CHO(g) \rightarrow CH_4(g) + CO(g)$$

If, however, the ethanal is heated to the same temperature with iodine vapour, the iodine catalyses the reaction; this latter reaction is first order with respect to both iodine and ethanal and has a lower activation energy than the reaction with ethanal alone.

(a) Explain the meaning of the terms which are underlined.

(b) Suggest a set of experiments by which you could confirm that the uncatalysed reaction is second order.

(c) Indicate briefly what experiments would be necessary to show that the reaction with iodine present has a lower activation energy than the decomposition of ethanal by itself.

In the last two sections of this Unit, we take a look at two theories which attempt to explain the observations obtained in chemical kinetics: (a) the collision theory, and (b) the transition state theory.

THE COLLISION THEORY

We have been assuming a simplistic version of the collision theory throughout the Unit: before a reaction can take place, molecules must collide.

You also know, from the section on activation energy and the effect of temperature of the rate of chemical reaction, that the colliding molecules must possess at least a certain energy - the activation energy - before they can react.

In this section, we go on to consider a third factor - the orientation of the colliding molecules.

Objectives. When you have finished this section you should be able to:

(32) state that, according to the collision theory, molecules must collide before they can react;

(33) state that before colliding molecules can react they must have an energy equal to, or greater than, the activation energy for the reaction;

(34) recognise that it is possible, using the collision theory, to calculate the number of 'fruitful' collisions occurring per unit time, under stated conditions, for a reaction;

(35) explain the significance of the steric factor, P.

Start by reading about the collision theory in your textbook(s). Look out for terms such as collision frequency (or collision number) and collision geometry (the steric factor concerned with the orientation of particles).

You know from Level One that, for a general reaction:

$$A + B \rightarrow products$$

$$rate = k[A]^m[B]^n$$

This means that, provided we choose reactions of the same order, comparing rate constants is a way of comparing the rates of those reactions at a given temperature.

You also know, from the section on the effect of temperature on reaction rates, that k is related to the activation energy by the Arrhenius equation:

$$k = Ae^{-E_a/RT}$$

Arrhenius derived this equation from a study of experimental results - it is an <u>empirical</u> equation. The collision theory produces an almost identical equation by means of <u>calculations</u> based on the theoretical model of gas consisting of spherical particles of a certain mass and size colliding together. For a second order gas reaction, the collision theory gives the expression:

$$k = Z^0 e^{-E_a/RT} \ldots\ldots\ldots\ldots(4)$$

where Z^0 is called the collision number and is related to the collision frequency of the particles. The collision frequency can be calculated from a knowledge of the number of particles in a given volume, their average speed and their size.

In the next exercise we give you values of the rate constants both experimentally determined and calculated from the collision theory for a series of reactions for which agreement is very good. The calculated values are obtained from the calculated value of Z^0 and the experimentally determined energy of activation. Study the table below and do the exercise which follows.

Table 14

Reaction	T/K	k(observed) /mol dm^{-3} s^{-1}	k(calculated) /mol dm^{-3} s^{-1}	k(obs)/k(calc)
$2HI(g) \rightarrow$ $H_2(g) + I_2(g)$	556	3.5×10^{-7}	5.2×10^{-7}	
$H_2(g) + I_2(g) \rightarrow$ $2HI(g)$	700	6.4×10^{-2}	14.0×10^{-2}	
$NO_2(g) + CO(g) \rightarrow$ $NO(g) + CO_2(g)$	500	0.55	1.7	
$2NOCl(g) \rightarrow$ $2NO(g) + Cl_2(g)$	300	1.5×10^{-5}	9.0×10^{-5}	

Exercise 40   Use the information in Table 14 to compare the observed and calculated values of k. Calculate the ratio of k(observed)/k(calculated) and enter the values in the last column of the table.

(Answers on page **88**)

As you have found in each case, the experimentally determined value is smaller than the calculated value. So how reliable is the collision theory? For many reactions, including some that take place in solution, the agreement is very poor. Agreement can be improved by refining the collision theory a little further. As well as needing enough energy to react, molecules must collide with the correct orientation. For example, in the reaction between CO and NO_2:

$$CO(g) + NO_2(g) \rightarrow CO_2(g) + NO(g)$$

it appears that the carbon atom of the CO must collide with one of the oxygen atoms on the NO_2 molecules so that a new bond may start to form between the carbon atom and an oxygen atom from NO_2:

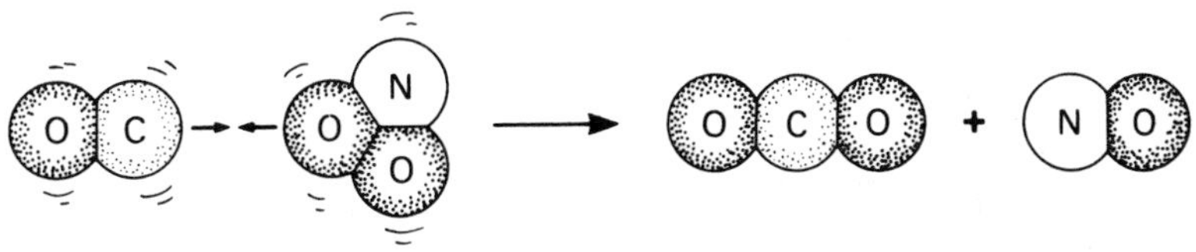

Fig.21.

If the carbon atom of CO were to collide with, say, the nitrogen atom of NO_2, there would be no reaction. The molecules would simply bounce apart again.

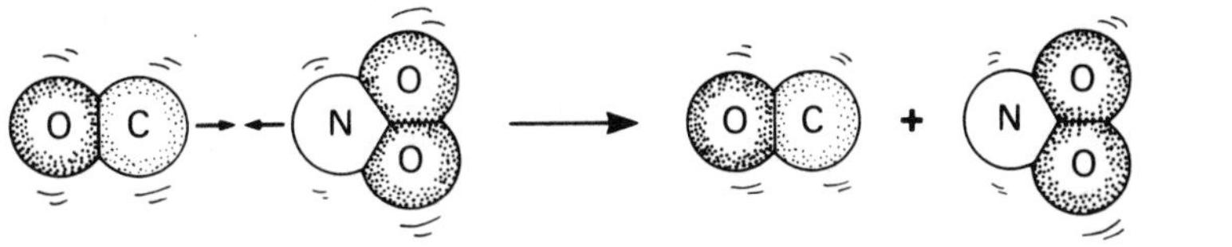

Fig.22.

This orientation correction is incorporated into equation (4) by an arbitrary constant P often referred to as the steric factor . Thus we can write:

$$k = PZ^\circ e^{-E_a/RT} \dots\dots\dots\dots(5)$$

If we compare this equation with the Arrhenius equation, the constant A is equal to PZ° and we can therefore obtain values for P for some reactions. In some cases, it has even been possible to see why reacting molecules of different structure give different values of P. However, since the collision theory does not provide an independent method of estimating P or E_a, it has little predictive value. Its strength lies in the simple pictorial model which it provides.

We end this section on the collision theory with an exercise concerned with the orientation of molecules.

Exercise 41   Consider the reaction

$$2AB(g) \rightarrow A_2(g) + B_2(g)$$

Assuming that the reaction occurs directly by means of simple collisions between AB molecules (i.e. bimolecular), draw diagrams to show the likely orientation of molecules:

(a) for a 'successful' collision which will lead to reaction;

(b) for an 'unsuccessful' collision.

(Answers on page 88)

We now consider another theory of reaction kinetics: the transition state theory. The main point about this theory is that it focuses attention on what happens to the reacting molecules after collision.

THE TRANSITION STATE THEORY

Objectives. When you have finished this section you should be able to:

(36) outline the transition state theory;

(37) apply the theory to a simple bimolecular reaction such as the hydrolysis of 1-iodobutane.

The transition state theory is covered in most physical chemistry text-books. You should have no difficulty in finding it. Read the section in at least one book.

In the transition state theory, attention is focused on the species existing at the point where the reactants are just about to transform into products. A species of this type is called an activated complex.

The basic assumption of the transition state theory is that the activated complex is in equilibrium with the reactant molecules, i.e.:

$$A + B \rightleftharpoons AB^{\#} \rightarrow \text{products}$$

where the symbol # refers to the activated complex in the transition state. The activated complex $AB^{\#}$ can decompose either into products or reactants again.

We now link the transition state theory to work you have already done on energy profiles.

Energy profiles and the transition state theory

Try the following exercise, in which you apply the transition state theory to the hydrolysis of 1-iodobutane.

Exercise 42 (a) Draw a simple energy profile diagram to illustrate the mechanism of hydrolysis of 1-iodobutane. Your diagram should not be to scale, but you can assume that the reaction is exothermic. You should include on the diagram the activated complex and the activation energy for the reaction.

(b) What would the activated complex be for the hydrolysis of 2-bromo-2-methylpropane?

(Answers on page 88)

The transition state theory formulates an equation which is analogous to the Arrhenius equation. The advantages of the transition state theory over the collision theory are that it automatically takes the steric factor into account and it allows direct calculation of activation energies in some cases. However, this theory is also unreliable for many reasons, but you are not expected to study it in any depth at A-level.

To help you focus your ideas on these two theories, we suggest you attempt the following Teacher-marked Exercise.

Teacher-marked Exercise — The collision theory and the transition state theory represent two different scientific models which the chemist uses in order to interpret experimental reaction rates. Give a concise account of each of these theories, and discuss the major similarities and/or differences that exist between them.

LEVEL TWO CHECKLIST

You have now reached the end of this Unit. In addition to what was listed at the end of Level One, you should now be able to:

(17) explain why a reaction mechanism can only be worked out from the rate equation for a reaction, not directly from the stoichiometric equation;

(18) state that most chemical reactions take place in a series of steps, each called an elementary step or reaction step;

(19) explain the meaning of the term molecularity;

(20) distinguish between the molecularity of a reaction step and the order of reaction as shown by the rate equation;

(21) identify the slowest step in a reaction as the rate-determining step;

(22) suggest a simple mechanism for a reaction from the rate equation and vice versa;

(23) use the rate equation for the hydrolysis of a halogenoalkane to work out a mechanism for the reaction;

(24) explain the effect of the carbon skeleton on the rate of hydrolysis of halogenoalkanes in terms of the stability of carbonium ions;

(25) state the meaning of the term activation energy and identify it on an energy profile diagram for a reaction;

(26) explain the effect of increased temperature on the rate of reaction in terms of the fraction of molecules with energy greater than the activation energy;

(27) state the Arrhenius equation which shows how the rate constant, k, changes with temperature;

(28) use a graphical method to obtain values for the activation energy from the Arrhenius equation;

(29) describe the difference between homogeneous and heterogeneous catalysis and give examples of each type;

(30) explain the action of a catalyst in terms of activation energy and reaction pathways;

(31) explain what happens in an autocatalytic reaction and give one example of this type of reaction;

(32) state that, according to the collision theory, molecules must collide before they can react;

(33) state that before colliding molecules can react they must have an energy equal to, or greater than, the activation energy for the reaction;

(34) recognise that it is possible, using the <u>collision theory,</u> to calculate <u>the number of 'fruitful' collisions</u> occurring per unit time, under stated conditions, for a reaction;

(35) explain the significance of the <u>steric factor,</u> P;

(36) outline the <u>transition state theory;</u>

(37) apply the theory to a simple <u>bimolecular reaction</u> such as the <u>hydrolysis of 1-iodobutane.</u>

Check that you have adequate notes before going on to the End-of-Unit Test.

END-OF-UNIT TEST

To find out how well you have learned the material in this Unit, try the test which follows. Read the notes below before starting.

1. You should spend about $1\frac{1}{2}$ hours on this test.

2. Hand your answers to your teacher for marking.

1. The rate of the reaction between peroxodisulphate ions and iodide
    ions in aqueous solution may be studied by measuring the amount
    of iodine formed after different reaction times. The stoichio-
    metric equation is:

$$S_2O_8{}^{2-}(aq) + 2I^-(aq) \rightarrow 2SO_4{}^{2-}(aq) + I_2(aq)$$

The graphs show the results of a kinetic investigation of this reaction.

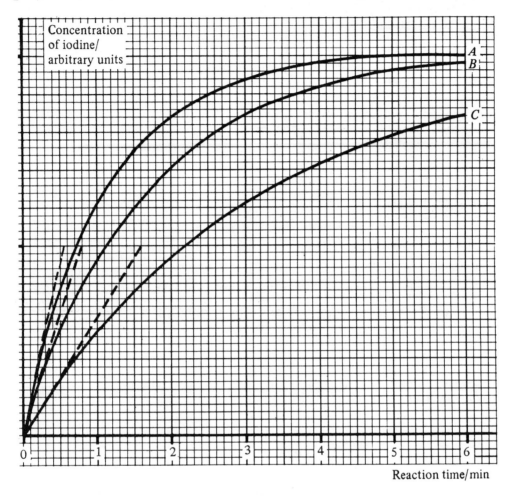

Reaction time/min

The experimental conditions were at a fixed temperature:

	Initial concentration of $S_2O_8{}^{2-}(aq)/mol\ dm^{-3}$	Initial concentration of $I^-(aq)/mol\ dm^{-3}$
Curve A	0.01	0.3
Curve B	0.01	0.2
Curve C	0.01	0.1

(a) Evaluate the <u>initial reaction rates</u> (given as $\Delta[I_2]/\Delta t$) for the
     three curves.   (3)

(b) (i)   With respect to which reactant concentration do these
           reaction rates vary?

     (ii) What is the order of the reaction with respect to this
           reactant?   (2)

(c) With reference to experimental curve A find the times required for the completion of:

  (i) one half of the reaction,

  (ii) three quarters of the reaction.

  In the light of these results what is the order of the reaction with respect to the second reactant? (4)

(d) (i) From your answers to parts (b) and (c), suggest an overall (2) rate equation for the reaction.

  (ii) What is likely to be the rate-determining step in this reaction? (2)

(e) Investigation of the kinetics of this reaction requires iodine concentrations to be determined. Outline a method by which this could be done. (3)

2. The Arrhenius equation, which involves the activation energy of a reaction, E, may be given in the forms

  either $k = Ae^{-E/RT}$ or $\ln k = \ln A - E/RT$

For the reaction

$$H_2(g) + I_2(g) \rightleftharpoons 2HI(g),$$

the values of k at 590 K and 700 K are 1.4×10^{-3} dm^3 mol^{-1} s^{-1} and 6.4×10^{-2} dm^3 mol^{-1} s^{-1} respectively. ($R = 8.3$ J K^{-1} mol^{-1})

(a) What do the symbols k, A, R, T represent? (2)

(b) Explain the meaning of the term activation energy. (2)

(c) Use an Arrhenius equation and the above data to calculate the activation energy for the reaction

$$H_2(g) + I_2(g) \rightarrow 2HI(g)$$ (5)

3. The diagram shows the distribution of the velocities of molecules in a gas at temperature T.

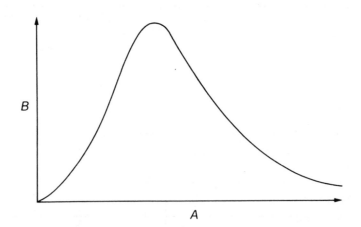

(a) The axes are labelled A and B. State what A and B represent. (2)

(b) Draw another curve on (a copy of) the diagram, showing a likely distribution at a higher temperature T_1. (2)

(c) How does the diagram now afford an explanation for the effect of increased temperature on the rate of a reaction? (2)

64

4. (a) *Homogeneous catalysts* for reactions may be found. Define each of the italicised words. (2)

   (b) Give one example of a homogeneous catalyst and specify a reaction which it catalyses. (2)

   (c)

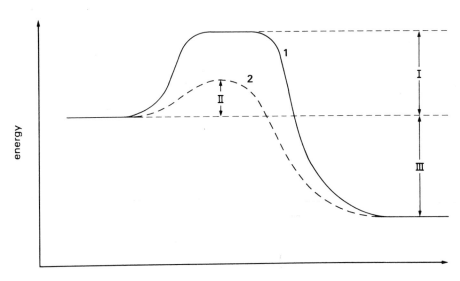

reaction co-ordinate

   In the diagram above, curve 1 shows the normal path for a particular reaction, while curve 2 shows the path in the presence of a catalyst. Define the energies marked I, II and III. (3)

5. An experiment was carried out to investigate the rate of reaction of an organic chloride of molecular formula C_4H_9Cl with hydroxide ions. The reaction was carried out in solution in a mixture of propanone and water with the following result:

Time elapsed /sec	Concentration of C_4H_9Cl/mol dm^{-3}	Concentration of hydroxide ions/mol dm^{-3}
0	0.0100	0.0300
294	0.0050	0.0250
595	0.0025	0.0225

   (a) Write a balanced equation for the reaction of an organic chloride of formula C_4H_9Cl with hydroxide ions. (2)

   (b) Suggest a reason why water alone is not used as the solvent in the experiment. (1)

   (c) (i) From the result given deduce an order of reaction. Explain your answer. (4)

       (ii) Write a rate expression for the overall reaction. (1)

       (iii) Suggest a mechanism for the reaction that would be consistent with your rate expression. (2)

   (d) Suggest a practical method by which it should be possible to follow the extent of the reaction. (2)

(Total 50 marks)

APPENDIX ONE

NOTES ON TANGENTS AND THEIR SLOPES

Drawing tangents

It might look easy to line your ruler up against the curve and draw a tangent 'by eye', but it is unlikely that you would get accurate tangents this way. We suggest two better methods in this Appendix to help you construct tangents accurately. You will need the following items: a sharp pencil and a ruler; either a small plane mirror or a glass rod; either a pair of compasses or a protractor.

The first step in drawing a tangent at a particular point on a curve is to draw a normal (perpendicular) at that point. We show you two methods - choose whichever is more convenient.

1. Drawing a normal to a curve using a mirror

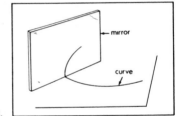 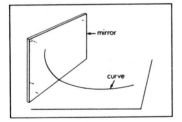 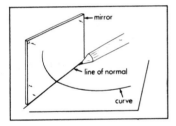

Fig.23.

Place a mirror across the curve so that you see the reflection of the curve in the mirror.

Move the mirror from side to side until the reflection of the curve in the mirror appears to be in a continuous line with the curve itself.

Draw a line along the edge of the mirror at this point. This is the normal to the curve.

2. Drawing a normal to a curve using a glass rod

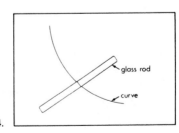 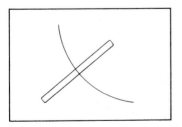 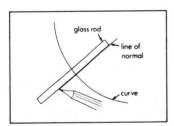

Fig.24.

Place the glass rod across the curve.

Move the rod sideways until the part of the curve seen through the rod appears to be in line with the other two parts.

Draw a line along the glass rod. This is the normal to the curve.

67

Having drawn a normal to the curve, you can easily draw a tangent at the point of intersection. Once again, we show you two methods.

1. Drawing a tangent using compasses

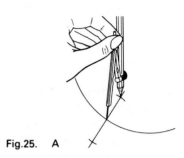  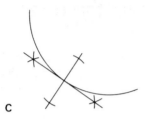

Fig.25.   A

B

C

Rest the point of the compasses on the intersection of the normal and the curve. Using a convenient radius, draw an arc that cuts the normal on either side.

Open the compasses until the radius is about 1½ times as big as it was. Rest the point on each arc in turn where it cuts the normal and draw four short arcs to intersect near the curve.

Using a ruler, draw a straight line joining the two crosses. This line is a tangent to the curve.

2. Drawing a tangent using a protractor (or a set-square)

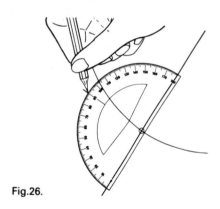

Line up the mark at the base of the protractor with the point where the normal crosses the curve. Make a mark opposite 90°. Do this each side, and join the two marks to get a tangent.

Fig.26.

It is important to draw tangents accurately because we can obtain useful information from measurements of their slopes. Slopes of lines can be positive or negative in sign as we now show.

Negative and positive slopes

The sign of a measured slope of a tangent indicates whether the property, Y, is increasing or decreasing with time, t. We show you how this sign is deduced with the aid of diagrams.

Figs. 27 and 28 show the two curves of the type you often meet in reaction kinetics showing the change in some quantity, Y, with time, t. A tangent is drawn in each case, and its slope is required in order to determine the rate of reaction.

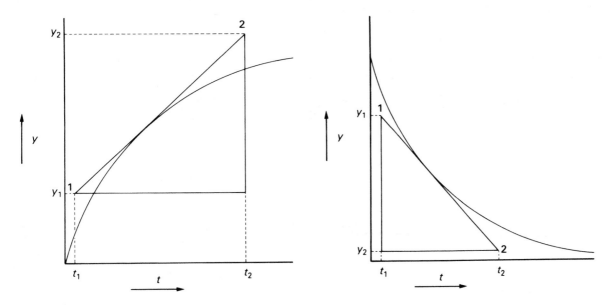

Fig.27.   A positive slope   Fig.28.   A negative slope

The slope is obtained by taking two points along the tangent at times t_1 and t_2, and noting the corresponding values of the measured quantity, Y_1 and Y_2.

The slope is defined as $\dfrac{\Delta Y}{\Delta t} = \dfrac{Y_2 - Y_1}{t_2 - t_1}$

In Fig. 27, Y (e.g. the volume of a gaseous <u>product</u>) is <u>increasing</u> with time, so that $Y_2 > Y_1$ and $Y_2 - Y_1$ is <u>positive</u>. The slope, therefore, is also positive.

In Fig. 28, Y (e.g. the concentration of a <u>reactant</u>) is <u>decreasing</u> with time, so that $Y_2 < Y_1$ and $Y_2 - Y_1$ is <u>negative</u>. The slope, therefore, is also negative.

Since the rate of reaction is always a positive quantity, it is necessary to change the sign of a negative slope when calculating rate from it. This concern about signs is particularly important when using the differential notation, as we show in the next section.

A note on 'differential notation'

In your reading you may have seen the symbol $\dfrac{d}{dt}$ written in front of a concentration term. For example, the rate equation for the decomposition of dinitrogen pentoxide could be written as

$$- \frac{d[N_2O_5]}{dt} = k[N_2O_5]$$

This is a mathematical notation meaning 'the rate of change of $[N_2O_5]$ with time'. Thus, the equation says that the rate of change of concentration of N_2O_5 is proportional to the concentration of N_2O_5. The negative sign indicates that the concentration is decreasing.

69

In practical terms, $\dfrac{d[N_2O_5]}{dt}$ is the slope of the concentration/time curve.

When rates are expressed in this shorthand notation, much information can be expressed with brevity. For example, for the reaction

$$2N_2O_5(g) \rightarrow 4NO_2(g) + O_2(g)$$

the rate of formation of nitrogen dioxide is four times the rate of formation of oxygen and twice as fast as the disappearance of dinitrogen pentoxide, i.e.

$$\frac{d[NO_2]}{dt} = \frac{4d[O_2]}{dt} \quad \text{and} \quad \frac{d[NO_2]}{dt} = \frac{-2d[N_2O_5]}{dt}$$

The negative sign is necessary because $[NO_2]$ is increasing while $[N_2O_5]$ is decreasing.

To see that you have understood this idea, try the following short exercise.

Exercise 43   Phosphine decomposes when heated, as follows:

$$4PH_3(g) \rightarrow P_4(g) + 6H_2(g)$$

At a given instant the rate at which phosphine decomposes is 2.4×10^{-3} mol dm^{-3} s^{-1}.

(a)   Express the rate of reaction in three different ways, using differential notation, and show the relationships between them.

(b)   What is the rate of formation of

(i) H_2,   (ii) P_4?

(Answers on page 88)

The great value of expressing rates of reaction in differential notation is that it enables us to express rate equations in another very useful form by means of the mathematical technique called integration. We give a brief survey of this in the next section - ask your teacher whether you need it for your syllabus.

INTEGRATED RATE EQUATIONS

We give here a very brief account, which you should fill out by reading the relevant sections in your textbook(s). We suggest you only do this if you have dealt with integration in mathematics.

Objectives.   When you have finished this section you should be able to:

(38)   write an integrated rate equation for a first order reaction;

(39)   obtain the rate constant for a first order reaction from a plot of log(concentration) against time;

(40)   show that the half-life of a first order reaction is constant;

(41)   write an integrated rate equation for a second order reaction;

(42)   obtain the rate constant for a second order reaction from a plot of time against 1/concentration.

First order reactions

You have already written a rate equation for the decomposition of dinitrogen pentoxide:

$$\text{rate} = k[N_2O_5]$$

Using differential notation, and writing c for $[N_2O_5]$, this becomes

$$-\frac{dc}{dt} = kc$$

Integrating gives $\ln c = -kt + I$ (I = integration constant.)

When $t = 0$, $c = c_0$ (the initial concentration) and $I = \ln c_0$. The equation thus becomes

$$\ln c = -kt + \ln c_0 \quad \text{or} \quad \log c = -kt/2.3 + \log c_0$$

This is an equation for a straight line and enables us to obtain the rate constant directly from concentration/time data by plotting $\log c$ against t and measuring the slope.

In the following exercises you can see how much easier this is than the method you learned in Level One, which involved <u>two</u> graphs and several intermediate calculations.

Exercise 44   Use the data in Table 1 on page 6 to show that the hydrolysis of 2,4,6-trinitrobenzoic acid is a first order reaction. Calculate the rate constant.

(Answer on page 88)

Exercise 45   The decomposition of dinitrogen pentoxide (N_2O_5) dissolved in tetrachloromethane (carbon tetrachloride) at 45 °C is first order. Using the concentrations of dinitrogen pentoxide and the times given, estimate by a graphical method the rate constant for the decomposition, stating the unit in which it is expressed.

Table 15

Time, t/s	0	250	500	750	1000	1500	2000	2500
c/mol dm^{-3}	2.33	1.95	1.68	1.42	1.25	0.95	0.70	0.50

(Answers on page 89)

In Level One you learned that first order reactions have a constant half-life. In the next exercise you confirm this mathematically by using the integrated rate equation.

Exercise 46   From the integrated rate equation for a first order reaction, obtain an expression for the time taken for the concentration to fall to half its initial value. How does this show that the half-life is constant?

(Answer on page 89)

Finally, we take a brief look at an integrated rate equation for second order reactions.

Second order reactions

We limit our discussion to two simple types:

$$A + A \rightarrow \text{products} \qquad [A] = c$$
$$A + B \rightarrow \text{products} \qquad [A] = [B] = c$$

Each of these gives the same rate expression:

$$-\frac{dc}{dt} = kc^2$$

Integrating gives $\qquad kt = 1/c - I$

When $t = 0$, $c = c_0$ $\quad \therefore \quad I = 1/c_0$ and the equation becomes

$$kt = \frac{1}{c} - \frac{1}{c_0} \qquad \text{or} \qquad t = \frac{1}{kc} - \frac{1}{kc_0}$$

This is an equation for a straight line and, once again, we can obtain the rate constant directly from concentration/time data. Try this in the next exercise - you should be able to see from the equation what graph to draw.

Exercise 47   Methyl ethanoate reacts with aqueous alkali according to the following equation:

$$CH_3CO_2CH_3(l) + OH^-(aq) \rightarrow CH_3CO_2^-(aq) + CH_3OH(aq)$$

The reaction may be followed by withdrawing samples at intervals and titrating with standard acid solution. The following results were obtained:

Table 16

Time/min	$[OH^-(aq)]/\text{mol dm}^{-3}$
3	7.40×10^{-3}
5	6.34×10^{-3}
7	5.50×10^{-3}
10	4.64×10^{-3}
15	3.63×10^{-3}
21	2.88×10^{-3}
25	2.54×10^{-3}

Determine a value for k, the rate constant for this reaction.

(Assume that the initial concentrations of methyl ethanoate and hydroxide ions were equal.)

(Answers on page 89)

72

APPENDIX TWO

'CLOCK' REACTIONS

In this appendix we deal with the theory of 'clock' reactions and we provide an alternative experiment to the iodination of propanone (Experiment 2).

The theory of 'clock' reactions

In a typical reaction, the early part of a concentration against time curve approximates to a straight line, as shown in Fig. 29 below:

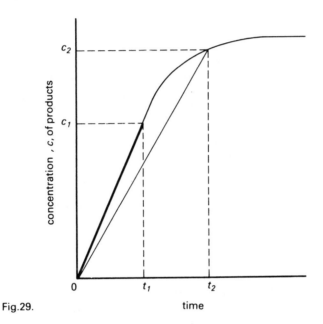

Fig.29.

If we choose any value of c (say c_1) which lies on this straight line, the initial rate of reaction is given by c_1/t_1. However, for a value of c (say c_2) beyond the straight part of the curve, the initial rate is greater than c_2/t_2.

In clock reactions, the initial rates of a series of reactions are obtained very simply by choosing a fixed value of c for all the reactions so that the rate = c/t. As long as c is constant, it need not necessarily be quantified, and we can take $1/t$ as a measure of the rate of reaction.

If you are doing the next experiment as an alternative to Experiment 2 and have not, therefore, done Experiment 3, we suggest that you read the introduction to Experiment 3 (page 50). This contains some useful information about clock reactions.

73

EXPERIMENT 5
A bromine 'clock' reaction

Aim

The purpose of this experiment is to determine the rate equation for the reaction between bromide and bromate(V) ions in aqueous solution.

Introduction

Bromide and bromate(V) ions in acid solution react according to the equation:

$$5Br^-(aq) + BrO_3^-(aq) + 6H^+(aq) \rightarrow 3Br_2(aq) + 3H_2O(l) \dots\dots\dots\dots\dots(1)$$

In order to follow the reaction, two other substances are added to the reaction mixture.

(a) A precisely known, small amount of phenol. This reacts immediately with the bromine produced, removing it from solution:

$$3Br_2(aq) + C_6H_5OH(aq) \rightarrow C_6H_2Br_3OH(aq) + 3H^+(aq) + 3Br^-(aq)\dots\dots\dots(2)$$

(b) Methyl orange solution, which is bleached colourless by free bromine:

$$Br_2(aq) + \text{methyl orange} \rightarrow \text{bleached methyl orange}\dots\dots\dots\dots\dots(3)$$
$$\text{(acid form: pink)} \quad \text{(colourless)}$$

As soon as all the phenol has reacted with bromine produced in reaction (1), free bromine will appear in solution and bleach the methyl orange. If the time taken for the methyl orange solution to be bleached is t, then the rate of reaction (1) is proportional to $1/t$.

In the experiment you study the effect on the rate of reaction (1) of varying the concentration of bromide ions, bromate (V) ions, and hydrogen ions in turn, with the concentrations of the others held constant. To save time, you could cooperate with other students and pool your results.

Requirements

safety spectacles
phenol solution, 0.0001 M C_6H_5OH
wash-bottle of distilled water
3 burettes and stands
measuring cylinder, 25 cm^3
potassium bromide solution, 0.010 M KBr
potassium bromate(V) solution, 0.0050 M KBrO$_3$
acidified methyl orange solution, labelled C, 0.001%
white tile
thermometer 0-100 °C
2 beakers, 100 cm^3
stopclock or watch
sulphuric acid, 0.01 M H$_2$SO$_4$
potassium bromate(V) solution, 0.20 M KBrO$_3$
methyl orange solution, labelled D, 0.001% in 0.40 M KBr

Procedure

A. Varying the concentration of bromide ions

1. Prepare the first pair of mixtures in two beakers, as specified in Table 17. Use burettes to measure the potassium bromide and phenol solutions and the water; use a measuring cylinder for the others.

Table 17

Beaker X		Beaker Y		
Volume of 0.01 M KBr /cm^3	Volume of H$_2$O /cm^3	Volume of 0.005 M KBrO$_3$/cm^3	Volume of solution C /cm^3	Volume of 0.00010 M phenol/cm^3
10.0	0	10.0	15.0	5.0
8.0	2.0	10.0	15.0	5.0
6.0	4.0	10.0	15.0	5.0
5.0	5.0	10.0	15.0	5.0
4.0	6.0	10.0	15.0	5.0
3.0	7.0	10.0	15.0	5.0

2. Have ready a copy of Results Table 6.

Results Table 6

Volume of Br$^-$(aq)/cm^3	10.0	8.0	6.0	5.0	4.0	3.0
Time, t/s						
$\frac{1}{t}$/10^{-2} s^{-1}						
Temperature/^{o}C						

Average temperature of solutions = ^{o}C

(Specimen results on page **90**)

3. Pour the contents of beaker X into beaker Y and start the clock. Mix the solutions by pouring from one beaker to the other, twice, and place the beaker containing the mixture on the white tile.

4. When the pink colour disappears, stop the clock and record the time in a copy of Results Table 6. (As you are looking for a disappearance of colour, this may need a little practice. If in doubt, repeat the reaction once or twice until you get consistent times.) Record the temperature of the solution.

5. Work through the rest of the mixtures in Table 17 in the same way, recording each result as you go.

B. Varying the concentration of bromate(V) ions

6. Follow a similar procedure to that for part A, but keep the volume of bromide solution constant at 10.0 cm^3 and vary the volume of bromate(V) solution as shown in Table 18.

Table 18

Beaker X		Beaker Y		
Volume of 0.005 M $KBrO_3$/cm^3	Volume of H_2O /cm^3	Volume of 0.01 M KBr /cm^3	Volume of solution C /cm^3	Volume of 0.00010 M phenol/cm^3
10.0	0	10.0	15.0	5.0
8.0	2.0	10.0	15.0	5.0
6.0	4.0	10.0	15.0	5.0
5.0	5.0	10.0	15.0	5.0
4.0	6.0	10.0	15.0	5.0
3.0	7.0	10.0	15.0	5.0

Record your results in a copy of Results Table 7.

Results Table 7

Volume of BrO_3^-(aq)/cm^3	10.0	8.0	6.0	5.0	4.0	3.0
Time, t/s						
$\frac{1}{t}$/10^{-2} s^{-1}						
Temperature/°C						

Average temperature of solutions =   °C

(Specimen results on page **90**)

C.   Varying the concentration of hydrogen ion

7.   For this part of the experiment you need different solutions, as stated in Table 19. Follow a similar procedure to that for part A.

Table 19

Beaker X			Beaker Y	
Volume of 0.01 M H_2SO_4/cm^3	Volume of H_2O /cm^3	Volume of 0.20 M $KBrO_3$/cm^3	Volume of solution D /cm^3	Volume of 0.00010 M phenol/cm^3
10.0	0	10.0	15.0	5.0
8.0	2.0	10.0	15.0	5.0
6.0	4.0	10.0	15.0	5.0
5.0	5.0	10.0	15.0	5.0
4.0	6.0	10.0	15.0	5.0
3.0	7.0	10.0	15.0	5.0

Record your results in a copy of Results Table 8.

Results Table 8

Volume of acid/cm^3	10.0	8.0	6.0	5.0	4.0	3.0
Time, t/s						
$\frac{1}{t}$/10^{-2} s^{-1}						
Temperature/°C						

Average temperature of solutions =   °C

(Specimen results on page 90)

Treatment of results

1. For each part of the experiment, plot a graph of $1/t$ against volume of the reactant under consideration. $1/t$ is proportional to the rate of reaction and the volume of reactant is proportional to the concentration, since the total volume is constant.

2. Deduce from each graph whether or not the reaction is first order with respect to the reactant under consideration.

3. If you think the reaction is <u>not</u> first order, plot another graph, as explained below.

    Suppose that, for a reactant A, rate = $k_1[A]^n$

    Under the conditions of this experiment, it follows that

    $1/t = k_2 V^n$ (V is the initial volume of reactant)

    $\therefore$ $\log(1/t) = n\log V + \log k_2$

    Plotting $\log(1/t)$ against $\log V$ should therefore give a straight line with slope n.

Questions

1. Write the rate equation for the reaction.

2. Qualitatively compare the rates of the three reactions stated in the introduction.

3. Why does the phenol solution need to be very dilute?

(Answers on page 91)

ANSWERS

Exercise 1

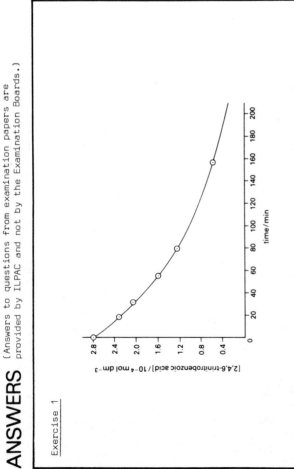

Graph: $[2,4,6\text{-trinitrobenzoic acid}]/10^{-4}\,mol\,dm^{-3}$ (y-axis, values 0.4 to 2.8) versus time/min (x-axis, 0 to 200).

Exercise 2

(a) Rate of reaction is greatest at time 0 and least at infinity, i.e. the rate decreases progressively with time.

(b) At any moment, the rate of reaction varies with the concentration of reactant. Since concentration of reactant decreases with time, rate of reaction decreases with time.

Exercise 3

Table 2

Time /min	Concentration /mol dm⁻³	Slope /mol dm⁻³ min⁻¹	Rate /mol dm⁻³ min⁻¹
10	2.50×10^{-4}	$-\dfrac{2.74 \times 10^{-4}}{112.5}$	2.44×10^{-6}
50	1.66×10^{-4}	$-\dfrac{2.49 \times 10^{-4}}{151.5}$	1.64×10^{-6}
100	1.04×10^{-4}	$-\dfrac{2.04 \times 10^{-4}}{199.5}$	1.02×10^{-6}
150	0.63×10^{-4}	$-\dfrac{1.58 \times 10^{-4}}{249}$	0.635×10^{-6}

Exercise 4

Graph: rate/$10^{-6}\,mol\,dm^{-3}\,min^{-1}$ (y-axis, 0.4 to 2.4) versus $[2,4,6\text{-trinitrobenzoic acid}]/10^{-4}\,mol\,dm^{-3}$ (x-axis, 0.2 to 2.4).

(a) Yes, the graph does pass through the origin. There can be no reaction (zero rate) if there is no reactant present (zero concentration).

(b) (i) The rate of reaction is proportional to the concentration of 2,4,6-trinitrobenzoic acid.

    (ii) rate $\propto [C_6H_2(NO_2)_3CO_2H]$ or   rate $= k\,[C_6H_2(NO_2)_3CO_2H]$

Exercise 5

(a) The reaction is first order with respect to 2,4,6-trinitrobenzoic acid.

(b) The reaction is also first order overall, since there is only one concentration term in the rate equation.

Exercise 6

Since rate $= k\,[C_6H_2(NO_2)_3CO_2H]$ a graph of rate against concentration of 2,4,6-trinitrobenzoic acid will be a straight line with a slope equal to k.

$$\text{slope} = \frac{\Delta(\text{rate})}{\Delta(\text{concentration})}$$

$$= \frac{2.44 \times 10^{-6}\,mol\,dm^{-3}\,min^{-1}}{2.50 \times 10^{-4}\,mol\,dm^{-3}} = \boxed{9.76 \times 10^{-3}\,min^{-1}}$$

Exercise 7

(a) From the graph from Exercise 1, the slope of a tangent to the curve at
time = 0 is:

$$\text{slope} = \frac{2.77 \times 10^{-4}\ \text{mol dm}^{-3}}{102.5\ \text{min}} = \boxed{2.70 \times 10^{-6}\ \text{mol dm}^{-3}\ \text{min}^{-1}}$$

This is the initial rate of reaction (at time = 0).

(b) To calculate the rate constant for each of the times listed in Table 2,
simply substitute values for rate and concentration in the rate
equation. The table below gives a summary of the values:

Time /min	Concentration /mol dm^{-3}	Rate /mol dm^{-3} min^{-1}	k/min^{-1}
0	2.77×10^{-4}	2.70×10^{-6}	9.75×10^{-3}
10	2.50×10^{-4}	2.44×10^{-6}	9.76×10^{-3}
50	1.66×10^{-4}	1.64×10^{-6}	9.88×10^{-3}
100	1.04×10^{-4}	1.02×10^{-6}	9.81×10^{-3}
150	0.63×10^{-4}	0.635×10^{-6}	10.1×10^{-3}

(c) Average value for k = $\boxed{9.86 \times 10^{-3}\ \text{min}^{-1}}$

Exercise 8

The value from the graph is likely to be more accurate. When you drew the
best straight line between the points on the rate against concentration
graph in Exercise 4, you were smoothing out some of the inaccuracies due to
experimental error - in effect taking an average of the rates and concentrations over the whole time range.

In Exercise 7 you averaged values from only five rates and concentrations,
which cannot be as accurate.

Exercise 9

For graph, see above right.

(a) Since the graph of rate against [N$_2$O$_5$] is a straight line, rate is
directly proportional to concentration of N$_2$O$_5$.
$$\therefore \text{rate} = k\ [\text{N}_2\text{O}_5]$$

(b) The reaction is first order with respect to N$_2$O$_5$.

(c) The value of the rate constant k is given by the slope of the graph,
which is:

$$\text{slope} = \Delta(\text{rate})/\Delta(\text{concentration})$$
$$= \frac{2.5 \times 10^{-5}\ \text{mol dm}^{-3}\ \text{s}^{-1}}{2.5\ \text{mol dm}^{-3}} = \boxed{1.0 \times 10^{-5}\ \text{s}^{-1}}$$

Exercise 9 (graph)

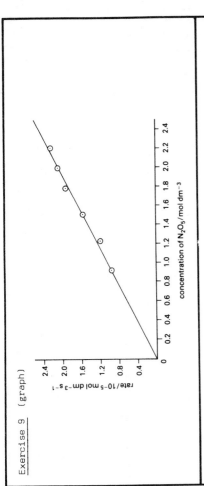

Exercise 10

(a) First order with respect to HgCl$_2$. Second order with respect to C$_2$O$_4$$^{2-}$.

(b) The reaction is third order overall.

Exercise 11

(a) The order is one with respect to C$_2$H$_4$ and 1.5 with respect to I$_2$.

(b) The overall order of reaction is 2.5.

Exercise 12

Since the reaction is third order overall, D could not be correct:

$$\text{rate} = k\ [\text{P}][\text{Q}]^3$$

as this shows a reaction which is fourth order overall.

Note that as [P]^0 = 1, B could be written as rate = k [Q]^3

Exercise 13

$$\text{rate} = k\ [\text{S}_2\text{O}_8{}^{2-}(\text{aq})][\text{I}^-(\text{aq})] \quad \therefore\ k = \frac{\text{rate}}{[\text{S}_2\text{O}_8{}^{2-}(\text{aq})][\text{I}^-(\text{aq})]}$$

Let rate = x mol dm^{-3} s^{-1}, [S$_2$O$_8{}^{2-}$(aq)] = y mol dm^{-3} and [I$^-$(aq)] = z mol dm^{-3}

$$\therefore\ k = \frac{x\ \text{mol dm}^{-3}\ \text{s}^{-1}}{(y\ \text{mol dm}^{-3})(z\ \text{mol dm}^{-3})} = \frac{x}{yz}\cdot\frac{\text{mol dm}^{-3}\ \text{s}^{-1}}{\text{mol}^2\ \text{dm}^{-6}} = \left[\frac{x}{yz}\right]\text{dm}^3\ \text{mol}^{-1}\ \text{s}^{-1}$$

i.e. the unit is $\boxed{\text{dm}^3\ \text{mol}^{-1}\ \text{s}^{-1}}$

Exercise 14

(a) Weighing, to find loss in mass. Collection of gas evolved (CO$_2$).

(b) Colorimetry. Collection of gas evolved (CO$_2$).

(c) Measuring change in conductivity.

(d) Dilatometry (reaction takes place with an increase in volume).

(e) Sampling and titration. Colorimetry. Conductivity measurement.

(f) Polarimetry.

Results Table 2

Time /min	Slope /cm³ min⁻¹	Rate /cm³ min⁻¹	$(V_\infty - V_t)$ /cm³
0	$\dfrac{219}{13.3}$	16.5	219
4	$\dfrac{214}{17.7}$	12.1	165
7	$\dfrac{202}{20.1}$	10.0	132
14	$\dfrac{150}{24.1}$	6.22	80
21	$\dfrac{88}{22.9}$	3.84	47

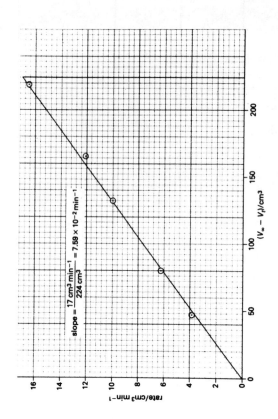

$$\text{slope} = \frac{17\ \text{cm}^3\ \text{min}^{-1}}{224\ \text{cm}^3} = 7.59 \times 10^{-2}\ \text{min}^{-1}$$

rate/cm³ min⁻¹ versus $(V_\infty - V_t)$/cm³

Experiment 1 – questions

1. Rate = $k\,[C_6H_5N_2{}^+Cl^-]$.
2. $k = 7.59 \times 10^{-2}$ min⁻¹ at 47 °C.
3. The initial gas escape can be neglected because we are interested in the volume change, $(V_\infty - V_t)$, e.g. if you had carried out the experiment and found that $V_\infty = 150$ cm³ and $V_t{}' = 50$ cm³ then $(V_\infty - V_t) = 100$ cm³.

   Suppose the volume of gas produced in the first four minutes was 10 cm³, then $V_\infty = 160$ cm³ and $V_t = 60$ cm³ but $(V_\infty - V_t)$ is still 100 cm³. Thus we can neglect the gas produced in the first four minutes.

Experiment 1. Specimen results and calculations.

Results Table 1

Time, t/min	0	1	2	3	4	5	6
Volume of N_2, V_t/cm³	0	14	28	41	54	65	76
$(V_\infty - V_t)$/cm³	219	205	191	178	165	154	143
Time, t/min	7	8	9	10	11	12	13
Volume of N_2, V_t/cm³	87	96	104	112	120	127	133
$(V_\infty - V_t)$/cm³	132	123	115	107	99	92	86
Time, t/min	14	15	16	17	18	19	20
Volume of N_2, V_t/cm³	139	145	150	155	160	164	168
$(V_\infty - V_t)$/cm³	80	74	69	64	59	55	51
Time, t/min	21	22	23	24	25		
Volume of N_2, V_t/cm³	172	175	177	181	184	219	
$(V_\infty - V_t)$/cm³	47	44	42	38	35	0	

Temperature of thermostat: 47 °C

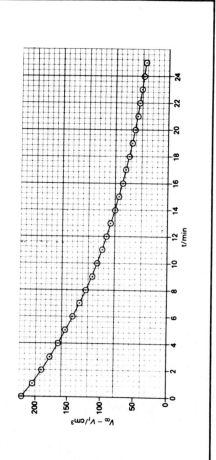

$V_\infty - V_t$/cm³ versus t/min

Exercise 18

(a) (i) Consider Experiments 1, 4 and 5, in which initial [B] is constant.

Doubling [A] doubles the rate, and tripling [A] triples the rate.

∴ with respect to A, reaction is first order

(ii) Consider Experiments 1, 2 and 3, in which initial [A] is constant.

Doubling [B] multiplies rate by 4 (2^2)

Tripling [B] multiplies rate by 9 (3^2)

∴ with respect to B, reaction is second order

(b) rate = $k[A][B]^2$

(c) Rearranging the expression in (b) gives $k = \dfrac{\text{rate}}{[A][B]^2}$

∴ $k = \dfrac{2.0 \times 10^{-3}\ \text{mol dm}^{-3}\ \text{min}^{-1}}{(0.100\ \text{mol dm}^{-3})^3} = 2.00\ \text{mol}^{-2}\ \text{dm}^6\ \text{min}^{-1}$

Exercise 19

(a) Consider Experiments 1, 2 and 3, in which initial [NO] is constant.

Doubling [H₂] doubles the rate, and tripling [H₂] triples the rate.

∴ with respect to [H₂], the reaction is first order i.e. $m = 1$

(b) Consider Experiments 4, 5 and 6, in which initial [H₂] is constant.

Doubling [NO] multiplies rate by 4 (2^2)

Tripling [NO] multiplies rate by 9 (3^2)

∴ with respect to [NO], the reaction is second order i.e. $n = 2$

Experiment 2. Specimen results

Results Table 3

Volume of 0.02 M I₂ solution/cm³	Volume of distilled water/cm³	[I₂(aq)] /10⁻³ mol dm⁻³	Meter reading (% ~~absorbence~~) (% transmission)
0.0	10.0	0.0	100.0
1.0	9.0	2.0	79.5
2.0	8.0	4.0	61.0
3.0	7.0	6.0	51.0
4.0	6.0	8.0	42.0
5.0	5.0	10.0	37.0

For an outline calibration curve see page 82.

Exercise 15

(a) The half-life of a reactant in a chemical reaction (or in radioactive decay) is the time taken for the concentration of a substance (or the amount, if solid) to fall to half its initial value.

(b) (i) The half-life of X is 10 mins.

(ii) First order.

(c)

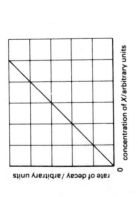

Exercise 16

(a)

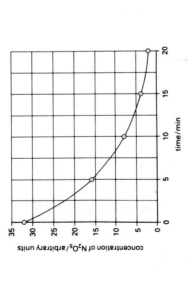

(b) rate = $k[N_2O_5]$

∴ $k = \dfrac{\text{rate}}{[N_2O_5]} = \dfrac{2.10 \times 10^{-5}\ \text{mol dm}^{-3}\ \text{s}^{-1}}{2.00\ \text{mol dm}^{-3}} = 1.05 \times 10^{-5}\ \text{s}^{-1}$

Exercise 17

Since the reaction is first order, the half-life is constant.

Half the benzenediazonium chloride decomposes in 40 mins giving 40 cm³ gas

A further half decomposes in a further 40 mins giving 20 cm³ gas

A further half decomposes in a further 40 mins giving 10 cm³ gas

Adding these figures shows that 70 cm³ of gas is evolved in 120 mins

Results Table 4

The graphs (top of page): meter reading (% transmission) vs concentration of iodine/10^{-3} mol dm⁻³ (calibration curve), and concentration of iodine/10^{-3} mol dm⁻³ vs time/min for curves (a), (b), (c), (d), (e), (f), (g).

	t = time/min	0	½	1	1½	2	2½	3	3½	4	4½	5	5½	6
a	% = % transmission	–	62.5	63.8	64.3	65.0	66.0	66.8	67.8	68.8	69.8	71.0	72.0	73.0
	I = [I₂(aq)]/10^{-3} mol dm⁻³	4.00	3.90	3.72	3.66	3.56	3.44	3.32	3.20	3.07	2.94	2.80	2.70	2.58
b	%	–	62.5	64.0	65.8	67.8	69.8	71.8	74.2	76.5	79.8	82.5	85.8	89.0
	I	4.00	3.90	3.70	3.46	3.20	2.94	2.72	2.42	2.18	1.83	1.55	1.25	0.95
c	%	–	65.0	67.0	69.8	72.5	76.0	79.8	83.8	88.0	93.0	97.5	–	–
	I	4.00	3.55	3.30	2.94	2.62	2.24	1.82	1.43	1.04	0.59	0.21	–	–
d	%	–	42.5	42.6	42.8	43.5	43.6	44.2	45.0	45.3	46.0	47.0	47.5	48.5
	I	8.00	7.75	7.70	7.59	7.40	7.37	7.18	6.97	6.88	6.75	6.50	6.40	6.20
e	%	–	79.0	80.0	80.5	81.9	83.0	84.1	85.5	87.0	88.5	90.0	91.8	93.5
	I	2.00	1.92	1.82	1.76	1.62	1.51	1.40	1.26	1.13	0.97	0.85	0.70	0.55
f	%	–	63.0	64.5	65.7	67.5	69.2	70.6	72.5	75.0	77.0	79.0	81.3	84.3
	I	4.00	3.82	3.63	3.46	3.23	3.02	2.84	2.62	2.34	2.15	1.92	1.68	1.38
g	%	–	63.4	65.8	68.3	71.5	74.5	78.0	81.9	85.0	88.3	93.3	98.0	–
	I	4.00	3.75	3.48	3.13	2.75	2.40	2.02	1.63	1.32	1.01	0.58	0.17	–

Initial rates of reaction are given by the slopes (with sign reversed) at time zero of the curves shown opposite.

(a) $\dfrac{(4.0 - 2.8) \times 10^{-3} \text{ mol dm}^{-3}}{6.0 \text{ min}}$ = 2.0×10^{-4} mol dm⁻³ min⁻¹

(b) $\dfrac{(4.0 - 1.8) \times 10^{-3} \text{ mol dm}^{-3}}{6.0 \text{ min}}$ = 3.7×10^{-4} mol dm⁻³ min⁻¹ ≈ 2 × (a)

(c) $\dfrac{(4.0 - 0.2) \times 10^{-3} \text{ mol dm}^{-3}}{6.0 \text{ min}}$ = 6.3×10^{-4} mol dm⁻³ min⁻¹ ≈ 3 × (a)

(d) $\dfrac{(8.0 - 6.7) \times 10^{-3} \text{ mol dm}^{-3}}{6.0 \text{ min}}$ = 2.2×10^{-4} mol dm⁻³ min⁻¹ ≈ 1 × (a)

(e) $\dfrac{(2.0 - 0.9) \times 10^{-3} \text{ mol dm}^{-3}}{6.0 \text{ min}}$ = 1.8×10^{-4} mol dm⁻³ min⁻¹ ≈ 1 × (a)

(f) $\dfrac{(4.0 - 1.9) \times 10^{-3} \text{ mol dm}^{-3}}{6.0 \text{ min}}$ = 3.5×10^{-4} mol dm⁻³ min⁻¹ ≈ 2 × (a)

(g) $\dfrac{(4.0 - 0.4) \times 10^{-3} \text{ mol dm}^{-3}}{6.0 \text{ min}}$ = 6.0×10^{-4} mol dm⁻³ min⁻¹ ≈ 3 × (a)

Orders of reaction

(a), (b) & (c) Initial values of [I₂(aq)] and [H⁺(aq)] are constant. Initial values of [CH₃COCH₃(aq)] and initial rates are both in ratio 1:2:3. Therefore, reaction is first order with respect to CH₃COCH₃.

(a), (d) & (e) Initial values of [CH₃COCH₃(aq)] and [H⁺(aq)] are constant. Initial values of [I₂(aq)] vary but initial rate is constant. Therefore, reaction is zero order with respect to I₂.

(a), (f) & (g) Initial values of [CH₃COCH₃(aq)] and [I₂(aq)] are constant. Initial values of [H⁺(aq)] and initial rates are both in ratio 1:2:3. Therefore, reaction is first order with respect to H⁺.

(a) The hydrogencarbonate reacts with the acid catalyst and effectively stops the reaction to enable the titration to be done.

(b) Since the iodine concentration is proportional to the volume of thio-sulphate solution used, the rate of change of iodine concentration is proportional to the slope of the graph. This is constant over the period illustrated.

(c) $\text{Rate} = \dfrac{\Delta V}{\Delta t} = \dfrac{(20-17)\ cm^3}{30\ min} = 0.10\ cm^3\ min^{-1}$

(d) The concentrations of propanone and acid are much greater than the initial concentration of iodine and can therefore be assumed to remain effectively constant. As the concentration of iodine falls, the rate of reaction remains constant; the reaction is therefore zero order with respect to iodine.

(e) Doubling the concentration should double the rate, i.e. $0.20\ cm^3\ min^{-1}$.

(f) & (g) There are two possible answers here. Either show the volume remaining constant over a period of 30 minutes, because the reaction, in the absence of a catalyst, proceeds too slowly to be measured; or show the volume decreasing slowly at first and then more rapidly over a longer period of time because there are a few hydrogen ions in any aqueous solution to catalyse the reaction and more are produced as the reaction proceeds.

The second alternative is theoretically sound but, in practice, the first corresponds to observation.

Exercise 21

(a) In each case the rate is obtained by substituting in the equation:

$$\text{rate} = k\,[H_2(g)][I_2(g)]$$

A. Rate $= 8.58 \times 10^{-5}\ mol^{-1}\ dm^3\ s^{-1} \times 0.010\ mol\ dm^{-3} \times 0.050\ mol\ dm^{-3}$

$= \boxed{4.29 \times 10^{-8}\ mol\ dm^{-3}\ s^{-1}}$

B. Rate $= 8.58 \times 10^{-5}\ mol^{-1}\ dm^3\ s^{-1} \times 0.020\ mol\ dm^{-3} \times 0.050\ mol\ dm^{-3}$

$= \boxed{8.58 \times 10^{-8}\ mol\ dm^{-3}\ s^{-1}}$

C. Rate $= 8.58 \times 10^{-5}\ mol^{-1}\ dm^3\ s^{-1} \times 0.020\ mol\ dm^{-3} \times 0.10\ mol\ dm^{-3}$

$= \boxed{1.72 \times 10^{-7}\ mol\ dm^{-3}\ s^{-1}}$

(b) Considering Experiments A and B, doubling the initial concentration of hydrogen at constant initial concentration of iodine doubles the rate of reaction.

Considering Experiments B and C, doubling the initial concentration of iodine at constant initial concentration of hydrogen doubles the rate of reaction.

Experiment 2.   Questions

1. The graphs show that the rate of reaction is directly proportional to the initial concentrations of both propanone and hydrogen ions, but is independent of the initial concentration of iodine. Thus, the reaction is first order with respect to propanone, first order with respect to hydrogen ions and zero order with respect to iodine. The rate equation is:

$$\text{rate} = k\,[CH_3COCH_3(aq)][H^+(aq)]$$

2. The overall order of reaction is two.

3. Hydrogen ions appear in the rate equation but are not reactants in the stoichiometric equation. On the other hand, iodine is a reactant but does not appear in the rate equation.

The rate of reaction must be determined by a step in the mechanism which involves propanone and hydrogen ions but not iodine.

4. Rate constants for this reaction at different temperatures have been quoted as follows:

Temperature/°C	15	20	25	30	35	40
Rate constant/10^{-3} mol^{-1} dm^3 min^{-1}	0.49	0.90	1.63	2.90	5.07	8.70

An average value at about 23 °C is obtained from our specimen results by dividing initial rates by initial concentrations as follows:

(a) $\dfrac{2.0 \times 10^{-4}\ mol\ dm^{-3}\ min^{-1}}{(0.40 \times 0.40)\ mol^2\ dm^{-6}} = 1.25 \times 10^{-3}$

(b) $\dfrac{3.7 \times 10^{-4}\ mol\ dm^{-3}\ min^{-1}}{(0.80 \times 0.40)\ mol^2\ dm^{-6}} = 1.16 \times 10^{-3}$

(c) $\dfrac{6.3 \times 10^{-4}\ mol\ dm^{-3}\ min^{-1}}{(1.20 \times 0.40)\ mol^2\ dm^{-6}} = 1.31 \times 10^{-3}$

(d) $\dfrac{2.2 \times 10^{-4}\ mol\ dm^{-3}\ min^{-1}}{(0.40 \times 0.40)\ mol^2\ dm^{-6}} = 1.38 \times 10^{-3}$

(e) $\dfrac{1.8 \times 10^{-4}\ mol\ dm^{-3}\ min^{-1}}{(0.40 \times 0.40)\ mol^2\ dm^{-6}} = 1.13 \times 10^{-3}$

(f) $\dfrac{3.5 \times 10^{-4}\ mol\ dm^{-3}\ min^{-1}}{(0.40 \times 0.80)\ mol^2\ dm^{-6}} = 1.09 \times 10^{-3}$

(g) $\dfrac{6.0 \times 10^{-4}\ mol\ dm^{-3}\ min^{-1}}{(0.40 \times 1.20)\ mol^2\ dm^{-6}} = 1.25 \times 10^{-3}$

Mean value 1.22×10^{-3} mol^{-1} dm^3 min^{-1}

Your values of the rate constant may differ considerably from those we have quoted, for a number of reasons (see Q5.). Nevertheless, you should be able to deduce the rate equation without too much difficulty.

5. The main sources of error may include the following.
   (a) Temperature variation during the experiment.
   (b) Variation in light output from the bulb in the colorimeter.
   (c) Sample tubes transmitting light differently. This may be due to
   (i) different tubes having different optical characteristics,
   (ii) the same tube being in different positions relative to the bulb, and behaving as a lens,
   (iii) drops of liquid or patches of dirt on the outside of the tube.
   (d) Solutions being prepared inaccurately.

Exercise 22

(a) Step 1 is bimolecular, step 2 is unimolecular, step 3 is bimolecular and step 4 is unimolecular.

(b) The mechanism does show H^+(aq) acting as a catalyst because it is necessary for the reaction to proceed as shown (step 1) but is regenerated (steps 2 and 4). However, unlike most catalysts, its concentration increases as the reaction proceeds - two H^+ ions are produced for each one used.

Exercise 23

(a) The individual steps do not add up to the overall equation:

$$ICl + H_2 \rightarrow HI + HCl$$

(b) The slow step does not agree with the rate equation. (rate $= k[ICl]^2$)

(c) The slow step does not agree with the rate equation. (rate $= k[ICl]$)

Exercise 24

(a) Step 1 is the rate-determining step since this is the slowest step.

(b) The molecularity of the rate-determining step has the same value as the overall order of reaction.

(c)

$$H{-}\overset{H}{\underset{H}{C}}{-}\overset{O}{C}{-}CH_3 + H^+ \rightarrow H{-}\overset{H}{\underset{H}{C}}{-}\overset{\oplus}{\underset{O{-}H}{C}}{-}CH_3 \qquad \text{Step 1 \quad slow}$$

$$H{-}\overset{H}{\underset{H}{C}}{-}\overset{\oplus}{\underset{O{-}H}{C}}{-}CH_3 \rightarrow H{-}C{=}\overset{}{\underset{O{-}H}{C}}{-}CH_3 + H^+ \qquad \text{Step 2 \quad fast}$$

$$H{-}C{=}\overset{}{\underset{O{-}H}{C}}{-}CH_3 + I_2 \rightarrow H{-}\overset{I}{\underset{H}{C}}{-}\overset{I}{\underset{O{-}H}{C}}{-}CH_3 + I^- \qquad \text{Step 3 \quad fast}$$

$$H{-}\overset{I}{\underset{H}{C}}{-}\overset{I}{\underset{O{-}H}{C}}{-}CH_3 \rightarrow H{-}\overset{I}{\underset{H}{C}}{-}\overset{}{\underset{O}{C}}{-}CH_3 + H^+ + I^- \qquad \text{Step 4 \quad fast}$$

$$CH_3COCH_3 + I_2 \rightarrow CH_2ICOCH_3 + H^+ + I^- \qquad \text{Overall equation}$$

Exercise 25

Possible mechanisms are:

$N_2O_5 \rightleftharpoons NO_2 + NO_3$ slow	or	$N_2O_5 \rightarrow NO_2 + NO_3$ slow
$NO_3 + NO_2 \rightarrow 3NO_2 + O_2$ fast		$NO_2 + NO_3 \rightarrow NO + O_2 + NO_2$ fast
		$NO_3 + N_2O_5 \rightarrow 3NO_2$ fast

Exercise 26

A possible mechanism is: $A + 2B \rightarrow AB_2$ slow

$AB_2 + B \rightarrow AB_3$ fast

Exercise 27

Possible mechanisms are:

$H_2 + 2NO \rightarrow 2NOH$ slow	or	$H_2 + 2NO \rightarrow N_2 + H_2O + O\bullet$ slow
$NOH + H_2 \rightarrow H_2O + NH$ fast		$O\bullet + H_2 \rightarrow H_2O$ fast
$NOH + NH \rightarrow H_2O + N_2$ fast		

(You need not be too concerned at this stage about postulating some rather unlikely-looking intermediates. However, avoid termolecular reactions as fast steps - they are bound to be very slow, e.g.

$$2NOH + H_2 \rightarrow 2H_2O + N_2 \text{)}$$

Exercise 28

(a) **Hydrolysis of bromomethane**

In experiments A, B and C, $[CH_3Br]$ is held constant; the effect of changing $[OH^-]$ is reflected in the rate. Thus, doubling the $[OH^-]$ doubles the rate and the reaction is first order with respect to OH^-.

In experiments D, E and F $[OH^-]$ is held constant and $[CH_3Br]$ varies. Doubling $[CH_3Br]$ doubles the rate, so the reaction is first order with respect to CH_3Br.

$$\therefore \text{ Rate } = k[CH_3Br][OH^-]$$

Hydrolysis of 2-bromo-2-methylpropane

In experiments A, B and C, $[(CH_3)_3CBr]$ is held constant and $[OH^-]$ varied. This has no effect on the rate. Therefore, the reaction is zero order with respect to OH^-; i.e. OH^- does not appear in the rate equation.

In experiments D, E and F, $[OH^-]$ is constant and $[(CH_3)_3CBr]$ varies. Doubling $[(CH_3)_3CBr]$ doubles the rate; therefore, the reaction is first order with respect to $(CH_3)_3CBr$.

$$\therefore \text{ Rate } = k[(CH_3)_3CBr]$$

(b) The formation of the activated complex must be the rate-determining step because it is bimolecular, which corresponds with the rate equation. The decomposition of the activated complex must be fast.

(c) $(CH_3)_3CBr \rightarrow (CH_3)_3C^\oplus + Br^-$ slow

$(CH_3)_3C^\oplus + OH^- \rightarrow (CH_3)_3COH$ fast

(d) S_N1 refers to a Nucleophilic Substitution reaction in which the molecularity of the rate-determining step is 1.

S_N2 refers to a Nucleophilic Substitution reaction in which the molecularity of the rate-determining step is 2.

Exercise 29

The presence of three bulky methyl groups and a large bromine atom around the central carbon atom prevents the approach of the hydroxide ion and the formation of an intermediate. This is known as 'steric hindrance'.

Exercise 30

(a)

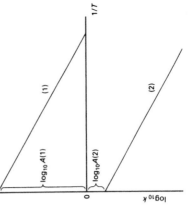

The graph is a straight line, which shows that the rate of reaction (as given by the slope) does not change with the concentration of ethylbenzene. This means that the reaction is zero order with respect to $C_6H_5C_2H_5$.

(b) The zero order of reaction means that $C_6H_5C_2H_5$ cannot appear in the rate-determining step.

(We suggest that this would be an adequate answer but you might wish to speculate further: e.g. the rate-determining step could be the formation of nitronium ions, which then react rapidly with ethylbenzene.

$$2HNO_3 \rightleftharpoons NO_2^+ + H_2O + NO_3^- \qquad \text{slow}$$

$$NO_2^+ + C_6H_5C_2H_5 \rightarrow C_6H_4NO_2C_2H_5 + H^+ \qquad \text{fast})$$

(c) The likely products are O_2N—$\langle$ring$\rangle$—C_2H_5 and $\langle$ring$\rangle$ C_2H_5, NO_2 (Hydrocarbons).
See Unit 01

Exercise 31

Energy is required to break bonds.

To allow new structures to develop, molecules may need to be deformed by violent collision and in this process nuclei approach more closely than they do in normal molecular contact. Energy is required to overcome the repulsive forces which operate at these distances. If the molecules do not have sufficient energy, they merely experience an elastic collision.

Exercise 32

(a)

activated complex

scale: 50 kJ mol⁻¹

$E_A = 250$ kJ mol⁻¹

$\Delta H_f^\circ = -164$ kJ mol⁻¹

$2N_2O(g)$

$2N_2(g) + O_2(g)$

potential energy

progress of reaction

(b) The activation energy of the back reaction
$$= (250 + 164) \text{ kJ mol}^{-1}$$
$$\boxed{= +414 \text{ kJ mol}^{-1}}$$

*It would be better to call this quantity an 'energy barrier' since it is not quite the same as the activation energy used in the Arrhenius equation. However, the distinction is rarely made at A-level.

Exercise 33

(a) Fraction of molecules with $E > 55.0$ kJ mol⁻¹ $= e^{-E/RT}$

$$= e^{-(55000 \text{ J mol}^{-1})/(8.31 \text{ J K}^{-1} \text{ mol}^{-1})(308 \text{ K})}$$

$$= e^{-21.5} = 4.60 \times 10^{-10}$$

Number $= L \times e^{-E/RT}$

$$= 6.02 \times 10^{23} \text{ mol}^{-1} \times 4.60 \times 10^{-10} = 2.77 \times 10^{14} \text{ mol}^{-1}$$

(b) $\dfrac{\text{number at 308 K}}{\text{number at 298 K}} = \dfrac{2.77 \times 10^{14}}{1.37 \times 10^{14}} = 2.02$

∴ twice as many molecules exceed the activation energy at 308 K as do at 298 K.

Exercise 34

(a) The variables in the equation

$$\log_{10} k = \log_{10} A - \frac{E_a}{2.3\,RT}$$

are k and T.

(b) $\log_{10} k$ is analogous to y, m to $E_a/2.3R$, x to $1/T$ and $\log_{10} A$ to c.

(c) The slope, $-E_a/2.3R$, is always negative and $1/T$ is always positive. $\log_{10} k$ may be positive or negative according to the magnitude of k (it is usually negative, corresponding to small values of k). The plot may take either of the two forms shown, with (2) the more probable.

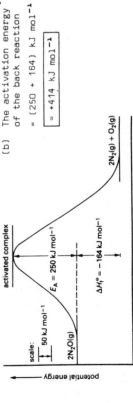

(d) The intercept on the vertical axis is equal to $\log_{10} A$. If the value of $\log_{10} A$ is obtained by reading the graph then A can be calculated. The slope of the straight line is equal to $-E_a/2.3\,R$. If the slope of the line is calculated from the graph then $E_a/2.3\,R$ can also be calculated, since R is a known constant.

Experiment 3. Specimen results

Results Table 5

Temperature/°C	30	36	39	45	51
Temperature, T/K	303	309	312	318	324
Time, t/s	204	138	115	75	55
$\log_{10}(1/t)$	-2.31	-2.14	-2.06	-1.88	-1.74
$\frac{1}{T}$/10^{-3} K^{-1}	3.30	3.24	3.21	3.14	3.09

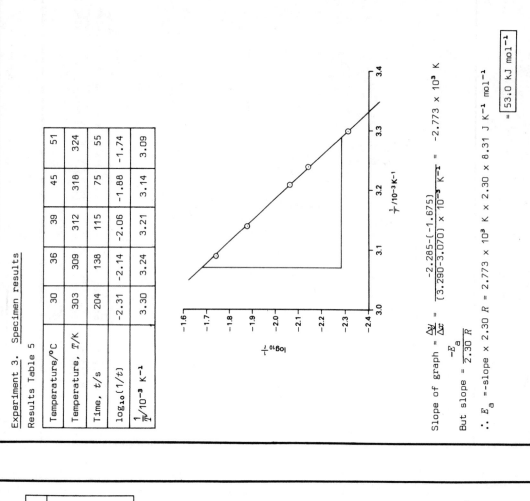

Slope of graph $= \dfrac{\Delta y}{\Delta x} = \dfrac{-2.285-(-1.675)}{(3.290-3.070) \times 10^{-3}\ \text{K}^{-1}} = -2.773 \times 10^{3}$ K

But slope $= \dfrac{-E_a}{2.30\ R}$

$\therefore E_a = -\text{slope} \times 2.30\ R = 2.773 \times 10^{3}\ \text{K} \times 2.30 \times 8.31\ \text{J K}^{-1}\ \text{mol}^{-1}$

$= \boxed{53.0\ \text{kJ mol}^{-1}}$

Exercise 35

(a)

T/K	$1/T$	k/dm^3 mol^{-1} s^{-1}	$\log k$
633	1.58×10^{-3}	1.78×10^{-5}	-4.75
666	1.50×10^{-3}	1.07×10^{-4}	-3.97
697	1.43×10^{-3}	5.01×10^{-4}	-3.30
715	1.40×10^{-3}	1.05×10^{-3}	-2.98
781	1.28×10^{-3}	1.51×10^{-2}	-1.82

Since $\log k = \dfrac{-E}{2.3\ R}\left(\dfrac{1}{T}\right) + \log A$

the slope of the graph $= -\dfrac{E}{2.3\ R}$

But the slope $= \dfrac{-4.00}{(1.61-1.20) \times 10^{-3}\ \text{K}^{-1}} = -9.76 \times 10^{3}$ K

$\therefore E = -2.3\ R \times \text{slope} = -2.3 \times 8.31\ \text{J K}^{-1}\ \text{mol}^{-1} \times -9.76 \times 10^{3}$ K

$= 1.86 \times 10^{5}\ \text{J mol}^{-1} = \boxed{186\ \text{kJ mol}^{-1}}$

(b) Writing k_1 and k_2 for the rate constants at 300 K and 310 K respectively:

$\log\left(\dfrac{k_2}{k_1}\right) = \log k_2 - \log k_1 = -\dfrac{E}{2.3\ R}\left(\dfrac{1}{310\ \text{K}} - \dfrac{1}{300\ \text{K}}\right)$

$= \dfrac{-186 \times 1000\ \text{J mol}^{-1}}{2.30 \times 8.31\ \text{J K}^{-1}\ \text{mol}^{-1}}(0.00323 - 0.00333)\text{K}^{-1} = 0.973$

$\therefore \dfrac{k_2}{k_1} = \text{antilog } (0.973) = \boxed{9.4}$

(c) $\dfrac{\text{kinetic energy at 310 K}}{\text{kinetic energy at 300 K}} = \dfrac{310\ \text{K} \times \text{constant}}{300\ \text{K} \times \text{constant}} = \boxed{1.03}$

(d) A very small increase in kinetic energy of a fixed mass of gas (such as HI) results in a great increase in the rate of reaction. This arises partly from the fact that collisions are more frequent at higher temperatures, but mostly from the fact that a greater proportion of the collisions have sufficient energy to cause a reaction to occur. The minimum energy for reaction to occur is called the activation energy.

Exercise 37

The list in the following table is incomplete, but illustrates the wide range.

Example of catalysed reaction	Catalyst	Type
$Zn(s) + 2H^+(aq) \rightarrow Zn^{2+}(aq) + H_2(g)$	$Cu(s)$	Heterogeneous
$2H_2O_2(aq) \rightarrow 2H_2O(l) + O_2(g)$	$MnO_2(s)$	Heterogeneous
	Enzyme in blood	Homogeneous
$CH_2{=}CH_2(g) + H_2(g) \rightarrow C_2H_6(g)$	$Ni(s)$	Heterogeneous
$CH_3CO_2C_2H_5(l) + H_2O(l) \rightleftharpoons CH_3CO_2H(aq) + C_2H_5OH(aq)$	$H^+(aq)/OH^-(aq)$	Homogeneous
$C_6H_6(l) + CH_3COCl(l) \rightarrow C_6H_5COCH_3(l) + HCl(g)$	$AlCl_3(s)$	Heterogeneous
$C_6H_6(l) + Br_2(l) \rightarrow C_6H_5Br(l) + HBr(g)$	$FeBr_3(s)$	Heterogeneous
$CH_3COCl(l) + H_2(g) \rightarrow CH_3CHO(l) + HCl(g)$	$Pd(s) + S(s)$	Heterogeneous
$C_2H_5OH(g) \rightarrow CH_2{=}CH_2(g) + H_2O(g)$	$Al_2O_3(s)$	Heterogeneous
$C_2H_5OH(g) \rightarrow CH_3CHO(g) + H_2(g)$	$Cu(s)$	Heterogeneous
$CH_3COCH_3(aq) + I_2(aq) \rightarrow CH_2ICOCH_3(aq) + HI(aq)$	$H^+(aq)$	Homogeneous
$2SO_2(g) + O_2(g) \rightleftharpoons 2SO_3(g)$	$V_2O_5(s)$	Heterogeneous
$N_2(g) + 3H_2(g) \rightleftharpoons 2NH_3(g)$	$Fe(s)$	Heterogeneous
$4NH_3(g) + 5O_2(g) \rightleftharpoons 4NO(g) + 6H_2O(g)$	$Pt(s)$	Heterogeneous

Exercise 38

(a) E_a for the forward reaction (catalysed) is 184 kJ mol^{-1}.
E_a for the back reaction (uncatalysed) is 236 kJ mol^{-1}.

(b) E_a for the forward reaction (catalysed) is 59 kJ mol^{-1}.
E_a for the back reaction (catalysed) is 111 kJ mol^{-1}.

(c) The enthalpy change is ± 52 kJ mol^{-1}.

Exercise 39

(a) Initial rate = slope at $t = 0 \simeq 6.3 \times 10^{-7}$ mol dm^{-3} s^{-1}

Rate at $t = 50$ s $\simeq 4.5 \times 10^{-6}$ mol dm^{-3} s^{-1}

Thus, the rate of reaction increases 7-fold over the first 50 seconds. This increase in the rate indicates that one of the products of the reaction is acting as a catalyst. The catalyst is likely to be the transition metal ions, $Mn^{2+}(aq)$.

(b) Two effects are operating during this reaction: the production of catalyst and the decrease in concentration of reactants. At the start of the reaction the first effect dominates; catalyst is being produced and speeds up the rate of the reaction as long as there is an adequate supply of reactant. Towards the end of the reaction, however, the second effect becomes more important. The concentration of reactants has fallen to a low level and so the rate of reaction decreases, even though there is an adequate supply of catalyst.

Exercise 36

Rate constants (k) are obtained by plotting loss in mass against time. Activation energy is obtained by plotting $\log k$ against $1/T$.

Experiment 1 at 0.5 °C			Experiment 2 at 13.5 °C			Experiment 3 at 25 °C		
Time /min	Mass /mg	Loss /mg	Time /min	Mass /mg	Loss /mg	Time /min	Mass /mg	Loss /mg
0	130	0	0	130	0	0	130	0
20	120	10	10	115	15	4	116	14
60	98	32	15	106	24	8	103	27
80	86	44	30	86	44	12	87	43

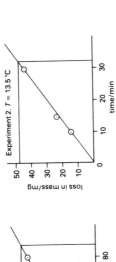

Experiment 1. T = 0.5°C

Experiment 2. T = 13.5°C

Experiment 3. T = 25°C

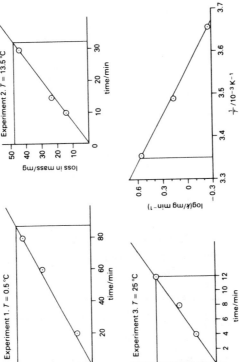

In each experiment, the straight line graph shows that the rate of loss of mass is constant. The rate constant, k, is the slope of the line.

1. $k = \dfrac{48.0 \text{ mg}}{88.0 \text{ min}} = \boxed{0.55 \text{ mg min}^{-1}}$

2. $k = \dfrac{48.0 \text{ mg}}{32.5 \text{ min}} = \boxed{1.48 \text{ mg min}^{-1}}$

3. $k = \dfrac{43.0 \text{ mg}}{12.0 \text{ min}} = \boxed{3.58 \text{ mg min}^{-1}}$

$k = B \times 10^{-E/2.3\,RT}$ (B is a constant)

$\therefore \log_{10} k = \log_{10} B - \left(\dfrac{E}{2.3\,R} \times \dfrac{1}{T}\right)$

Slope of graph $= \dfrac{(-0.30 - 0.58)\text{mg min}^{-1}}{(3.67 - 3.35) \times 10^{-3} \text{ K}^{-1}} = -2.75 \times 10^3 \text{ K} = \dfrac{-E}{2.30\,R}$

$\therefore E = 2.30 \times 8.31 \text{ J K}^{-1} \text{ mol}^{-1} \times 2.75 \times 10^3 \text{ K} = \boxed{52.6 \text{ kJ mol}^{-1}}$

If the cobalt were not rotated, the rates of reaction (and hence the rate constants) would be slightly smaller, due to the time taken for $S_2O_8^{2-}$ ions to diffuse towards the metal surface. Activation energy would be unaffected.

Exercise 43

(a) $-\dfrac{d[PH_3(g)]}{dt} = 4 \times \dfrac{d[P_4(g)]}{dt} = \dfrac{2}{3} \times \dfrac{d[H_2(g)]}{dt}$

(b) (i) $\dfrac{d[H_2(g)]}{dt} = -\dfrac{3}{2} \times \dfrac{d[PH_3(g)]}{dt} = -\dfrac{3}{2} \times (-2.4 \times 10^{-3} \text{ mol dm}^{-3} \text{ s}^{-1})$

$= \boxed{3.6 \times 10^{-3} \text{ mol dm}^{-3} \text{ s}^{-1}}$

(ii) $\dfrac{d[P_4(g)]}{dt} = -\dfrac{1}{4} \dfrac{d[PH_3(g)]}{dt} = -\dfrac{1}{4} \times (-2.4 \times 10^{-3} \text{ mol dm}^{-3} \text{ s}^{-1})$

$= \boxed{6.0 \times 10^{-4} \text{ mol dm}^{-3} \text{ s}^{-1}}$

Exercise 44

Let c = concentration of 2,4,6-trinitrobenzoic acid.
If the reaction is first order,

$$\log c = -kt/2.30 + \log c_0$$

t/min	0	18	31	55	79	157
c/10^{-4} mol dm^{-3}	2.77	2.32	2.05	1.59	1.26	0.58
$\log (c/\text{mol dm}^{-3})$	-3.56	-3.63	-3.69	-3.80	-3.90	-4.24

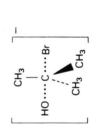

Since the graph is a straight line, the reaction is first order. The slope of the graph = $-k/2.30$

$$\therefore k = -2.30 \times \frac{-4.30-(-3.56)}{(165-0)\text{ min}} = \boxed{1.03 \times 10^{-2} \text{ min}^{-1}}$$

Exercise 40

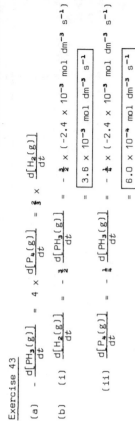

Reaction	T/K	k(observed) /mol dm^{-3} s^{-1}	k(calculated) /mol dm^{-3} s^{-1}	k(obs)/k(calc)
2HI(g) → H$_2$(g) + I$_2$(g)	556	3.5×10^{-7}	5.2×10^{-7}	0.67
H$_2$(g) + I$_2$(g) → 2HI(g)	700	6.4×10^{-2}	14.0×10^{-2}	0.46
NO$_2$(g) + CO(g) → NO(g) + CO$_2$(g)	500	0.55	1.7	0.32
2NOCl(g) → 2NO(g) + Cl$_2$(g)	300	1.5×10^{-5}	9.0×10^{-5}	0.17

Exercise 41

(a) For 'successful' collisions, molecules are likely to be aligned with A and B atoms facing each other.

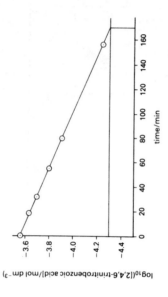

(b) Three orientations which would result in 'unsuccessful' collisions are shown below, but there are many others.

Exercise 42

(a)

(b)

88

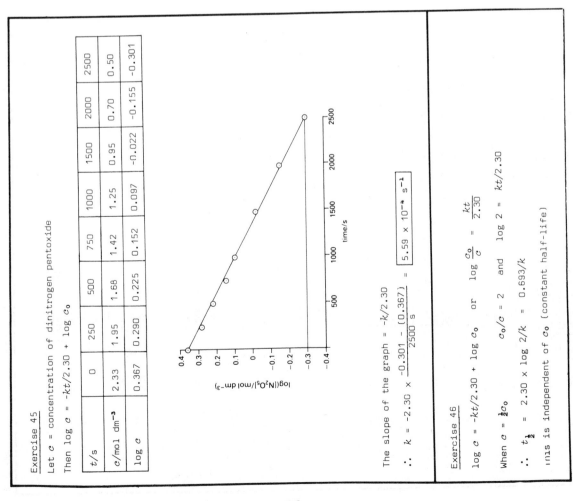

Exercise 45

Let c = concentration of dinitrogen pentoxide

Then $\log c = -kt/2.30 + \log c_0$

t/s	0	250	500	750	1000	1500	2000	2500
c/mol dm⁻³	2.33	1.95	1.68	1.42	1.25	0.95	0.70	0.50
$\log c$	0.367	0.290	0.225	0.152	0.097	-0.022	-0.155	-0.301

The slope of the graph = $-k/2.30$

∴ $k = -2.30 \times \dfrac{-0.301 - (0.367)}{2500}$ s = $\boxed{5.59 \times 10^{-4} \text{ s}^{-1}}$

Exercise 46

$\log c = -kt/2.30 + \log c_0$ or $\log \dfrac{c_0}{c} = \dfrac{kt}{2.30}$

When $c = \tfrac{1}{2}c_0$ $c_0/c = 2$ and $\log 2 = \dfrac{kt}{2.30}$

∴ $t_{\frac{1}{2}} = 2.30 \times \log 2/k = 0.693/k$

This is independent of c_0 (constant half-life)

Exercise 47

Let c = [OH⁻(aq)]

Then $t = 1/kc - 1/c_0$

t/min	3	5	7	10	15	21	25
c/10⁻³ mol dm⁻³	7.40	6.34	5.50	4.64	3.63	2.88	2.54
$1/c$/dm³ mol⁻¹	135	158	182	216	275	347	394

The slope of the graph = $1/k$

∴ $k = 1/\text{slope} = \dfrac{(406 - 140) \text{ mol}^{-1} \text{ dm}^3}{(26.0 - 3.4) \text{ min}^{-1}}$ = $\boxed{11.8 \text{ mol}^{-1} \text{ dm}^3 \text{ min}^{-1}}$

Experiment 5. Specimen results

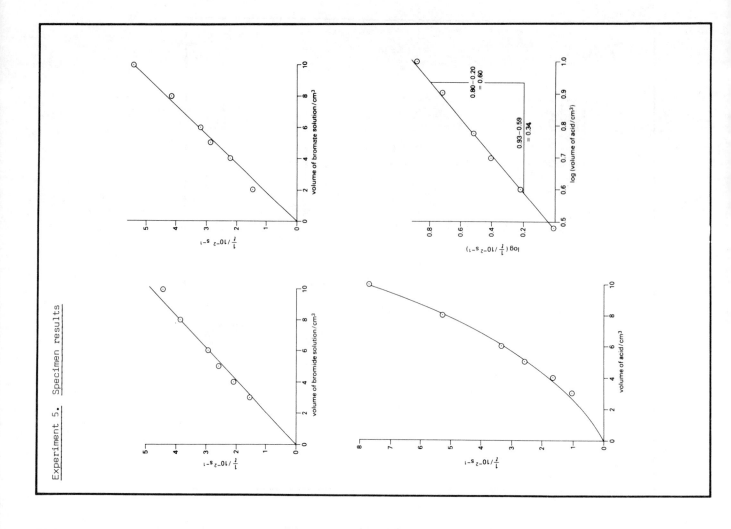

Experiment 5. Specimen results

Results Table 6

Volume of Br⁻(aq) cm³	10.0	8.0	6.0	5.0	4.0	3.0
t/s	22.5	26.0	34.0	37.5	48.0	65.0
$\frac{1}{t}/10^{-2}\ s^{-1}$	4.44	3.85	2.94	2.67	2.08	1.54
Temperature/°C	21.0	21.5	21.5	21.5	22.0	22.0

Average temperature of solutions = 21.5 °C

Results Table 7

Volume of BrO_3^-(aq)/cm³	10.0	8.0	6.0	5.0	4.0	3.0
t/s	18.5	24.0	31.0	35.0	45.0	69.0
$\frac{1}{t}/10^{-2}\ s^{-1}$	5.41	4.17	3.23	2.86	2.22	1.45
Temperature/°C	21.5	22.0	21.5	21.5	22.0	21.5

Average temperature of solutions = 21.5 °C

Results Table 8

Volume of acid/cm³	10.0	8.0	6.0	5.0	4.0	3.0
t/s	13.0	19.0	30.0	39.0	60.0	97.0
$\frac{1}{t}/10^{-2}\ s^{-1}$	7.69	5.26	3.33	2.56	1.67	1.03
Temperature/°C	21.5	21.5	21.5	22.0	21.5	21.5

Average temperature of solutions = 21.5 °C

Graphs 1 and 2 are straight lines (see opposite page).
Therefore the reaction is first order with respect to Br⁻(aq) and to BrO_3^-(aq).
Graph 3 is not a straight line. (Note that the line must pass through the origin since, when $V = 0$, $t = \infty$ and $1/t = 0$.)
Plotting log 1/t against log (Volume of acid/cm³):

$\log(\frac{1}{t}/10^{-2}\ s^{-1})$	0.886	0.721	0.522	0.408	0.223	0.013
$\log(V/cm^3)$	1.000	0.903	0.778	0.699	0.602	0.477

Slope of graph 4 = $\dfrac{0.60}{0.34}$ = 1.8

This suggests that the reaction is second order with respect to H⁺(aq).
(However, it is possible that there could be two mechanisms operating at
once, which could give a fractional order of 1.8.)

Experiment 5. Questions

1. Rate = $k[Br^-(aq)][BrO_3^-(aq)][H^+(aq)]^2$

2. The reaction producing bromine:

$$5Br^-(aq) + BrO_3^-(aq) + 6H^+(aq) \rightarrow 3Br_2(aq) + 3H_2O(l)$$

is slow compared with the other two. This allows the bromine to be removed from solution as soon as it is formed, by the reaction with phenol:

$$3Br_2(aq) + C_6H_5OH(aq) \rightarrow C_6H_2Br_3OH(aq) + 3H^+(aq) + 3Br^-(aq)$$

Similarly, the indicator reaction is fast so that as soon as the phenol has been used up free bromine will bleach its colour.

3. The phenol solution needs to be dilute in order to restrict the main reaction to its early stages, when the concentration-time curve is almost linear. Within this region the average rate of reaction (which is what you measure in a clock reaction) approximates to its initial rate.

Note on the mechanism

You may be surprised to find a reaction which is fourth order overall; this seems to imply that four molecules collide in the rate-determining step - a most unlikely occurrence!

A possible mechanism is:

$H^+(aq) + Br^-(aq) \rightleftharpoons HBr(aq)$ fast

$H^+(aq) + BrO_3^-(aq) \rightleftharpoons HBrO_3(aq)$ fast

$HBr(aq) + HBrO_3(aq) \rightarrow$ products   slow

Then rate = $k[HBr(aq)][HBrO_3(aq)]$

But $[HBr(aq)] \propto [H^+(aq)][Br^-(aq)]$

and $[HBrO_3(aq)] \propto [H^+(aq)][BrO_3^-(aq)]$ (from consideration of equilibrium constants)

∴ rate = $k'[Br^-(aq)][BrO_3^-(aq)][H^+(aq)]^2$